LAKE SUPERIOR'S NORTH SHORE
AND ISLE ROYALE

Kate Crowley and Mike Link

Additional photography by
Dominique Braud   Daniel J. Cox   Dick Dietrich
Bob Firth   Steve Kuchera   Michael Magnuson
John and Ann Mahan   L. David Mech   Ronald Morreim
Joe Niznik   Lynn Rogers   Paul Sundberg

VOYAGEUR PRESS

Dedicated to the memory of Thomas Savage,
who loved the North Shore

89 90 91 92 93   5 4 3 2 1

Library of Congress Cataloging-in-Publication Data

Crowley, Kate.
  Lake Superior's North Shore and Isle Royale / Kate Crowley and Mike Link.
    p.   cm.
  ISBN 0-89658-115-2 : $14.95
  1. Superior, Lake, Region — Description and travel — Guide-books.
2. Natural history — Superior, Lake. Region — Guide-books. 3. Isle
Royale (Mich.) — Description and travel — Guide-books. 4. Natural
history — Michigan — Isle Royale — Guide-books. I. Link, Michael.
II. Title.
F552.C76 1989
917.74'90443--dc20   89-14782
                                                       CIP

Published by Voyageur Press, Inc.
123 North Second Street
Stillwater, MN 55082 U.S.A.
In Minn 612-430-2210
Toll Free 800-888-9653

Voyageur Press books are also available at discounts in bulk quantities for premium or sales-promotion use.
For details contact the Marketing Manager.

Please write or call for our free catalog of natural history publications.

CONTENTS

INTRODUCTION

BY MIKE LINK

Writing about the North Shore is a labor of mixed emotions. Our series is called Wilderness Books, yet except for Isle Royale National Park, the North Shore does not contain a designated wilderness area, nor do people go to the shore seeking wilderness experiences. Is this classification wrong? We don't think so.

An official designation does not make an area a wilderness, nor does the lack of designation make a place less wild. The wooded North Shore contains wild, untamable rivers and canyons, numerous parks, part of Superior National Forest, long backpack and cross-country ski trails, and remote lands. In addition, a water wilderness dominates everything we do in this region.

If Lake Superior is not "wild," we dare not use the adjective on any location. The huge storm-generated waves crashing against lava buttresses, the ice blocks singing out in the night as they grate against one another, the glimmering moonbeams across a hundred miles of open water are primitive experiences, earth experiences—wilderness sensations.

We also wrestle with the regional name, North Shore. That's what everyone calls it, but a geographer might argue that it is really the northwest shore; near Nipigon, which is really the beginning of the "north" shore, our story ends.

But there is a northerly trend to everything on this side of the lake. Lake Superior has been described as a drawn bow, the south side being the string and the north side the cedar bow. If so, the arrow it propels will go straight toward the North Pole, following the expanse of boreal forests that extend from the lake's rocky ridges.

The lake is a jumping-off point for true north. Here you feel that once you leave Highway 61, you can wind your way to Hudson's Bay without encountering another human being. It is part of a country that claims adjectives like *rugged*, *awesome*, and *hardy*.

Our book is a personal view of this area. It is a combination of many experiences and many different trips. We have chosen to take a trail of memories from Duluth to Thunder Bay because all of our experiences are rooted to individual locations, and the locations are the real stimuli for memories.

We have not written a guidebook, nor have we written a textbook. We want to share our feelings, and enrich yours.

The Superior Hiking Trail meanders over rocky ridges and through hardwood and conifer forests. (B. Firth)

In winter, snowy owls haunt the frozen Duluth harbor, subsisting on rodents that live near the port and railroad tracks. (J. Niznik)

WILD DULUTH

MINNESOTA POINT by Mike Link

Beyond the Apostle Islands the lake is open, and shelter along the south coast is hard to find when storms strike. There are some nice sand beaches where rivers enter Superior, but much of the shoreline is steep banks of red clay. In 1679, when Daniel Greysolon, Sieur du Luth, rode the wave crests of Superior in a canoe, the sight of the massive sweep of beach and dunes at the mouth of the St. Louis River must have brought a sense of relief.

To the north, a massive dark ridge of tall timber and rock angled to the southwest. In the south, a broad flat plain led away from the shore. This was clay country, the old lake bed deposits of glacial Lake Duluth, and the dense forest obscured all but the immediate landscape.

The canoes didn't have to land on the sand beach. This is the end of the lake, but there is a natural break between the barrier beaches that come off each shore.

The St. Louis River wanders around the northern ridges and cuts its valley into the old lake clays. After a turbulent ride through ancient slates and graywackes in Jay Cooke State Park, the river slows down and forms a broad, low wetland.

Greysolon would have followed a meandering course southwest until he found the site where he established his encampment. In 1792, Jean Baptiste Cadotte established the first non-Indian settlement in Minnesota near here—a post called Fond du Lac.

The valley of the St. Louis has undergone many changes since the Sieur du Luth's days. Ore and ocean ships have replaced the birchbark vessels of commerce. Two cities have replaced two forts, and Lake Superior has been divided among two countries and three states.

The bison, the caribou, and the wolverine are no longer part of Minnesota's ecology, but the St. Louis River estuary is still rich in natural diversity. Large migratory concentrations of wood ducks and swans are here, and a good variety of breeding birds. There is even a population of the same fur bearer, the beaver, that attracted the voyageurs in the first place.

To many people the harbor of Duluth and Superior seems part of Lake Superior, but it is really part of the river. The river carries sediments from upstream, and the storms of Lake Superior transport sediments toward the port. Lake currents, wind-driven waves, and river current all meet here, cancel each other out, and deposit large amounts of sand.

All this accumulation either fills the harbor, which keeps the dredges busy, or adds to the barrier beaches, which are known as Wisconsin Point and Park Point. They are ribbons of sand, beaches backed by dunes that slope toward the river. In Minnesota, the long arm of the point has numerous homes, a canal, and even an airport.

While change has been dramatic, so has continuity, in the form of wings. Migrating shorebirds touch down on the beach, while planes land on the opposite side of the dunes. The airport landing strip is often white with gulls and roseate terns. Savannah sparrows nest in the grass along the runway.

As waves wash in and out, sanderlings scurry back and forth. They look like an indecisive group of bathers, who want to be next to the water but aren't sure they want to get their feet wet.

A flock of birds suddenly flash by and land in a solitary part of the beach, where they take pebbles and turn them over, just as their name implies. The ruddy turnstones are plump birds, with a branching black throat patch and reddish wings. In flight they are a maze of red, black, and white patterns across wings and body.

Large, dull-colored shorebirds take wing and expose brilliant white-and-black patterns as they call out their name: "*willet*." Stout-billed plovers, usually heavier-bodied and singular, are here too. Birds such as the ruff, dunlin, and Hudsonian godwit (which only the serious birder can identify quickly, because of their rarity in Minnesota), also wander these beaches during migration.

The most common shorebird is the spotted sandpiper. With a thoroughly dotted neck and body, orange bill, and olive wings, it tends to be more conspic-

Duluth Harbor is a mix of massive ore boats and tiny shorebirds. (M. Link)

In Duluth Harbor, Lake Superior and the St. Louis River meet. Dredges work constantly to keep the harbor safe for both recreational and commercial boating. (S. Kuchera)

uous than other shorebirds. It nests in the sparse beach grass and stays all summer. Its flight is usually short, and its wings seldom get above a flat plane, making the bird look like it is straining to stay airborne. When it alights, the tail bobs up and down like a vehicle with broken springs and shocks.

The shorebirds are late spring migrants and begin their return flights in August. They are on their "home" grounds only a couple of months each year for breeding.

Birders, that segment of society that hunts feathered prey with binoculars rather than guns, tend to be most excited by shorebirds and warblers, because both groups of birds demand a lot of attention to details. Both are difficult to observe well, but have interesting lifestyles and many variations. For birders, Minnesota (Park) Point is a bonanza.

Behind the dunes is a forested area, which is a concentration point for warblers and other migrants who are thwarted by the open water of Lake Superior. These birds follow the south shore until they reach the barrier beach forests, and then they make their break to the north. The result is one of Minnesota's most important birding hotspots.

Fortunately, Park Point is protected as a natural area, and the picnic and play development is limited. But Duluth sits in such a rich natural-history area that even where limited development has taken place, some wildlife still exists. Across the harbor in the even more developed Port Authority area, the common terns have chosen to nest in a large colony.

Common terns are sand nesters, and very few places have the right conditions for them. Beaches are one of our nation's most critical habitats. In Minnesota, Lake of the Woods, Leech Lake, Mille Lacs, and Lake Superior are the only places where big breeding colonies of terns exist, and each of these big lakes has a limited number of suitable nesting sites. In addition, the increase in herring gulls (due to their adaptation to humans) has created avian competition on the breeding grounds.

Not everyone is happy about the terns in Duluth. In 1979, an article said that they were "an embarrassment to dignitaries in the harbor, during breeding," and efforts were made to establish a new nest site on Hearding Island. The terns are aggressive breeders and dive-bomb all intruders, even dignitaries.

The harbor makes up an interesting struggle between nature and development. In some ways it demonstrates the potential that we have for coexisting with other species if we take the time to understand our impacts. On the other hand, it represents the adaptability of nature.

In winter, the harbor can be a maze of jumbled ice blocks where pressure ridges heave and crack. Here snowy owls stand in an imitation Arctic. They are most easily observed when they sit on lamp and telephone poles, but they are more of a ground bird, since the Arctic lacks trees. They stand or lie among the ice blocks and disappear as their black feathers break up their solid outlines, causing them to blend in with oth-er lines and shadows. For their prey, rodents from railroading activities replace lemmings in this environment.

Pigeons substitute for the gyrfalcon's prey as this cliff-dwelling northern falcon perches on the top of the grain elevators during many winters. Both of these Arctic birds have made remarkable substitutions for their normal home environment.

The harbor is a marvelously complex system deserving much more protection and appreciation, but it is not the only indication of Duluth's rich ecological heritage.

Black bear warnings are issued when the berry crops are bad and the bruins look to garbage for extra fall sustenance. One restaurant is named for a black bear with gourmet tastes that came right in the restaurant window.

Most communities can watch squirrels and chipmunks. Some other cities have white-tailed deer in wild sections of the community. But I won't forget the moose that stepped off a lawn in Duluth to cross the road in front of me. It simply walked across to the next lawn and disappeared into someone's backyard.

HAWK RIDGE by Kate Crowley

Hawk Ridge sounds like an upscale condominium development, and no doubt hungry developers have cast a desirous eye on this 115-acre section of property perched eight hundred feet above Duluth and the great lake.

Luckily, since 1972 it has been set aside as a nature reserve under a trust agreement with the city of Duluth and the Duluth Audubon Society, which manages it. In 1973, two hundred adjacent acres were purchased as a buffer zone for the nature reserve.

Following the Skyline Drive (if you're paying attention and not driving too fast), you will see a wooden sign, directing you down one mile of dirt road to Hawk Ridge. On sunny September weekends, it is easy to follow the steady flow of vehicles going in and out.

Visiting on a bright, warm fall day, you find a feeling of a street carnival at the ridge. Cars park along both sides of the road, people wander back and forth, and some set up lawn chairs to eat picnic lunches while they overlook the hazy expanse of lake and horizon. Groups of people stand in clusters, craning their necks as they peer through binoculars at little black specks high in the sky.

Two "migrations" are occurring at the same time: From the south, a steady stream of vehicles bearing birders comes to witness the migration of thousands of birds of prey streaming from the north. The bird migration begins in mid-August and doesn't end until December, but the peak numbers generally occur near the middle of September, which often coincides with peak autumn colors.

The Minnesota Ornithologists Union and a group known as Friends of Hawk Ridge support, organize, and promote activities related to the annual migration, and Hawk Ridge in particular. Approximately one

Not all the birds seen at Hawk Ridge are high in the sky. Some, like the evening grosbeak, may be found at eye level in a nearby shrub. (D. Cox)

thousand hours are spent by experienced, highly skilled birders, who make the daily counts. They must be able to identify a red-tailed hawk silhouetted against a grey sky, hundreds of feet overhead. They must make quick counts of numerous black shapes swirling and circling forward above the ridge and determine how many species are in the cluster.

On a good day—sunny, with a west or northwest wind—as many as twenty thousand birds may be counted. Cloudy, rainy days with south or east winds slow the process. One participant who has been involved with the count over the years said the weather "turns out good about every other year."

The ridge acts as a funnel for birds moving down from the north. Lake Superior is a massive body of water to cross, and it is safer to follow the coastline. The ridge also channels updrafts that send the birds soaring quickly to the south.

Nineteen species of hawks have been seen at Hawk Ridge, although it is only recently that the peregrines and merlins (a small falcon) have begun to reappear in larger numbers. In 1987, thirty-two merlins were seen in one day. That type of sighting makes all the time and effort worthwhile for the workers.

On one trip, Mike and I sat back-to-back in the sun on the exposed, lichen-covered gabbro, waiting for our group, who were hiking on some of the reserve's two and one-half miles of trails. In the shrubbery, we heard small "*chip*" sounds and caught brief glimpses of small greenish-yellow birds, more commonly known as "frustrating fall warblers."

It was a perfect day to be on the ridge. There is much sumac on this portion, and the rich scarlet leaves formed part of the color quilt. Birch leaves twisted in the breeze, glinting gold in the sun, and the oaks added to the rustling with their crisp russet leaves. Every once in awhile, we would hear someone call out the name of a bird and we would grab our binoculars and search the sky for the prize. I will always have a large amount of respect and a small bit of skepticism for the counters' ability to distinguish and separate such small dark shapes into distinct species.

As we walked back to the roadside, where the majority of the people stand, we heard the excited cry, "Peregrine!" Binoculars snapped to attention and focused on the slope below the road. I saw it as it sped out of my field of vision. Not a good, slow look, but one that gave me a real appreciation of its streamlined

form and famous speed.

On a Saturday afternoon, when the crowd greatly outnumbered the migrating birds because of poor wind conditions, naturalist Kim Eckert seized the opportunity to do a little informal educating. He reminded me of a roadside magician as he stood on a slope in front of a growing crowd, holding a hawk in each hand.

Occasionally, the nearby banding station will send some birds to the counting area for visitors to see. Kim held the birds up high and asked the crowd if anyone knew what species they were. After a few tries, someone called out, "Sharp-shins."

"Right. You've seen quite a few of these flying by today. They have real long, skinny legs. That's why they're called sharp-shins.

"Now, how old are they?"

A tougher question, one that only a well-trained birder could answer. Someone suggested, "Immature." That was right, but they were of different ages. The one in Kim's left hand was this year's hatch and could be identified as such by its yellow eye and brown streaks on the wings and brown back. The other bird was a one-year-old, identified by its orange eye and rusty bars.

"Now, what sex are they?" asked Kim.

Both were females, but he said you really needed a male to hold next to them to show the size difference.

The two birds were anxious to be on their way, so he let one go and it shot up, circled, and flew off. Kim let a visitor hold the other bird before releasing it. When the woman opened her hand, the free bird skimmed over the crowd, causing heads to duck, and then it too was gone.

It was not that long ago that Hawk Ridge was used by "hunters" as an easy location to take potshots at migrating raptors. Through the efforts of concerned locals and city officials, a special area has been protected. As a result, so have the birds who are following an age-old flight plan.

Hawk Ridge may not have any endangered plants or animals within its boundaries, but it is a wonderfully wild place, where people can gather and look together at the birds in the sky and wish them well on their journey south.

Ice blocks, like huge crystal building blocks, became an instant playground for Mike and his students. (B. Firth)

KNIFE RIVER

BY MIKE LINK

It was a clear winter day in March and I had a group of foreign students with me. Our objective was to get a feeling for the flavor of the North Shore, but we were limited to one day and we didn't want to spend the entire day in the vehicle. Many times, I plan a trip's itinerary with specific stops to accomplish the feeling that I want to convey, but sometimes a free spirit has to take hold. There are days when spring slides into the winter season and the sun's warmth reaches beyond the skin level.

This was one of those moments when the ice sheets that take tentative possession of the lake are broken into shards and stacked in crackling ridges along the shoreline as the big water reasserts its dominance. The sun glistened on the water and the blue seemed more vivid because it had been locked in an icy shell for so long. I craved the blueness in the same way that I crave spring's green and the bird's fresh songs.

Near Duluth, the ice blocks were large, and stacked in a massive pressure ridge that we could scale. They were crystal building blocks, and the child in us made us scramble over the slippery pieces, seeking the glimmer of sunshine and the inspiration of exotic shapes. Closer to the town of Knife River, where the road sweeps along the cobblestone shore and then moves inland, the blocks were smaller and the ridges were stacked on the cobbles.

We stopped and looked at the scene, the sweeping vista of shoreline arching northeast, the green-blue Wisconsin shore across the lake, and gulls singing and careening along the beach.

"Bird people" debate whether a watcher with binoculars can tell the difference between the Thayer's gull and the herring gull. Until a few years ago, there was no debate because they were considered the same bird. Then scientists split the two, separating an Arctic gull from its widespread cousin. The Arctic Thayer's gull became a new possibility for life lists, and the field ornithologist wanted to join the lab technicians in the pleasure of a new discovery.

Birders wrote of observations, and academicians "harrumphed." For most of the bird world, this mattered very little, but here on the shores of Lake Superi-or, Arctic birds often enjoy balmy visits, and the Thayer's gull is known to be here.

I have no arguments with either group, but on this day, the sunlight was so perfect that details were part of every image. There was no haze; it was a day of awareness and sharpness. Days like this hone our perception of the world. They give clarity to hazy existence and allow us illumination and focus.

Near shore sat a gull, a large gull with a white head and a yellow beak, with the familiar red patch on the lower mandible. It could have been a herring gull, but something wasn't quite right. The National Geographic field guide says that the Thayer's gull can be distinguished "by more uniform body plumage, shorter, stubbier bill, and lack of contrasting dark secondaries." That is too subjective for me, and I would have a hard time calling a bird a new "lifer" on those kinds of marks. Still, I didn't think this bird looked like all the beggars I have seen on shore and while sailing. Peterson's guide added that the Thayer's gull has pinker legs, rather than the flesh-colored legs of the herring gull. It may seem crazy, but these legs did seem pinker. Then I saw the eye ring, just as the book showed it, a narrow red band between the brownish iris and the head's white plummage. Only in this light would I dare make such a claim. But make it I do. I believe I saw a Thayer's gull.

The gull was not exciting to my students; it was a discovery for the returning adventurer, the person who has had time to experience many of the shore's special qualities. The newcomers were overwhelmed by the grandeur, the vista, and the diverging shorelines.

We drove into Knife River and purchased smoked fish. We bought lake trout, a treasure of the deep cold waters, smoked by rich wood until the flesh breaks into bite-size pieces. Then we took the trout, some crackers, and fruit juice to the beach, where we broke off pieces of ice "candles" (old ice that has broken into vertical slivers) for our cups of juice. We sat contentedly munching and drinking, warmed by the sun and soothed by the clear notes of shifting and disintegrating ice.

13

WHITE PINES— ENCAMPMENT

BY MIKE LINK

Each trip north reacquaints me with the white pines near the Encampment River. Each ride through the cathedral draws my attention to the shape and size of the grove. These are magnificent trees, the northeastern equivalent of the redwood. White pines won't grow to the size of the mountain giants, but then the northeastern woods have always possessed a more subtle beauty.

The white pine charms by bulk and diversity of form. They are not spired like the great spruce and fir, and they are not symmetrical like the red pine. Instead, each white pine is individually sculpted by wind and sun. Individual branches may grow out of proportion to their ranks along the trunk and their relative ages. They may even usurp the position of the main trunk. When crowns are broken, the branches trend upward, straining to reach the sun in competition with the other branches, and often two or more will become dominant, giving the crown the appearance of an entire grove perched on a single pedestal.

Five needles in a bunch, five letters in the word *white*. How many times have I and other instructors used this device for teaching neophytes how to identify the white pine? How often have I told people that the large trees marching across the ridges are white pines and that you can tell them from a distance because their branches look like arms laden with needles, rather than fuzzy fingers surrounded by them?

White pines don't stir just my imagination, either. They were the "king's trees" in the colonies, the tall, straight mast that moved the British fleet against the Spanish and the other challengers in the Atlantic. The king's representatives had imagination too. They saw the large trees with full sails.

Describing the trees even brings out the poet in the botanist. In Rosendahl's *Trees and Shrubs of the Upper Midwest*, he describes the older pines as having "strong, irregular, ascending branches forming an open irregular crown." I can picture that.

There was a time when the glaciers erased what lived here and began the sequence of life all over again. During the last 15,000 years the Encampment River

site was under the waters of the glacial Lake Duluth, was the site of a tundra garden, and may have seen a succession of other forest types.

Those who stick probes deep into the accumulated peat of the bogs have studied pollen grains laid down over the centuries, which present a succession from the glacial ice to the forests of today. In this time capsule we see the region moving from tundra (short plants on a permafrost soil) to boreal spruce forests, the same type of forest that rings the tundra in northern Canada. Jack pine and red pine were the next species to take root and dominate, followed by paper birch and alder growths. Then about seven thousand years ago, during a warm period, the white pine came in and grew to dominance, out-competing the colder-climate species.

For about three thousand years, the white pine was the king of the forest, not the king's tree. It grew well then for the same reasons that it grows well know, and it faced the same limitations that it faces now.

It has the most exacting requirements for growing conditions of all the pines. The cones of the white pine are the largest, and they take two years to ripen into viable seeds. The cones are not produced in abundance every year; instead the trees have a regular cycle of three to five years between bumper crops. The long cones are the result of a May flowering, when the pollen spreads on the wind in yellow dust storms. Fifteen months later, if the right conditions prevail, the cone falls to repopulate the forest.

The right conditions mean mineral soil, lack of competition, and adequate moisture. The seeds must find a sunny area of fresh mineral soil (for example, a burn) without competitors to shade the seedling.

For the first three to five years of growth the plant needs enough snow to cover it entirely during the severe freezing months. The young plant puts most of its energy into the development of roots, not aerial parts.

As a baseball fan, I am enamored of the statistics and percentages that tell me about the various possibilities and potential that exist in the game. As a biologist, I

A cascade and pool along the Encampment River. (B. Firth)

15

am just as fascinated by the combinations that exist in the natural world. Just think of all these cycles and conditions coming together, then add summer droughts, wildfires, diseases, and grazing animals. It makes me all the more appreciative of the white pine's beauty.

Nature is always "full"—is always at capacity. The addition of a new plant or animal means the elimination of another. Substitution of one plant for another means altering an entire food web. Shifting populations, changing communities—nature is never lacking, but it is always changing, whether the cause is human activity or not.

After the white pine's peak, four to seven thousand years ago, the climate underwent changes in temperature and moisture. The cooler, moister climate encouraged jack pine and cedar growth, while discouraging the white pine. The cedars that share the area around Encampment with the white pines also decreased after a period of dominance, because of their sensitivity to fire. The jack pine flourished, and the black spruce increased in the wetlands, replacing the cedars.

Then the big change came, the shift in population of the most devastating species. Loggers came to Minnesota from the denuded forests of the east, and a vision of vast wealth spread out before them. The white pine industry would have died out in the United States but for the discovery of the vast forests of the interior. Lumbermen came to these shores, to the rivers and the inland lakes, and made proclamations that sound ridiculous today. "We'll never run out of white pine, the supply is endless." "We'll never be able to cut all there is in this region." How giddy we become when we are confronted with abundance.

But commerce is more than the dreams of the timber cruiser. It is the greed and energy of business, the faceless energy of industry applied to a single purpose. The white pine fell, massive logs clogged large rivers, and the lumber industry had a glut of beautiful white boards.

Gone were the trees that could grow for five hundred years and reach heights of over two hundred feet. Replacing them were aspens, which regenerate quickly, spread rapidly, and out-compete new white pine seedlings.

Thoreau observed the fresh-cut white pine logs of his forests and the purplish sap that concentrates along each cut end. From the purplish bruise, the sap would "distill perfectly clear and crystalline tears, colorless and brilliant as diamonds, tears shed for the loss of a forest in which is a world of light and purity, its life oozing out."

The North Shore was lumbered hard; trees fell in great quantities, and only a few survived. This grove at the Encampment River is one of the reminders, one of the links with our forest history.

The loggers were a colorful part of our history and are still an important part of local economies, but like all industries, they need restrictions and limits. It is much more important for us to see the remaining virgin stands than for someone to convert them into glossy paper or paneling. We cannot regrow 500-year-old trees, we can only start young trees that may one day replace them.

I have never been in the homes along the Encampment. I have not walked the woods, because they are privately owned, but I can still bask in their beauty, along with every other driver on the Shore. The fact that they survive is what is important to me.

The great Wisconsin botanist John Curtis wrote the following description in his 1959 classic, *The Vegetation of Wisconsin*: "If there is one tree which can be used to exemplify the northern forests, it is the white pine. . . . When the vacation-bound traveler from the hot and steamy cities of the south, sees his first white pine, he knows that he is entering the 'northwoods'. . . . white pine is truly a sign of pleasant summer days and cool nights."

The white pine's range extends farther than Curtis's picturesque description allows, but the tree remains the symbol of both our ecology and our history here on the North Shore.

A white pine spared from the loggers' saws and a seedling for the future. (S. Kuchera)

SPLIT ROCK

BY KATE CROWLEY

Along the North Shore, Split Rock stands alone as an example of a lighthouse style that fulfills our romantic images of the lights that mark rugged landscapes and roaring waters.

It was no small task to build this structure at the top of a 124-foot cliff accessible only by water. A huge derrick was installed on the rock and used to haul 310 tons of building material up to the site. Brush was cleared and then dynamite was used to blast out the foundations for the buildings. It is amazing that no lives were lost, nor was anyone even injured, during this dangerous phase of construction.

My first visit to the lighthouse occurred one February with Mike and a group of foreign students. We drove them up the North Shore to share some of the state's most dramatic scenery. It had been a mild winter and there wasn't enough snow for skiing or snowshoeing, so we decided to do the next best thing and take them cross-country hiking.

We parked the van in the lot across the road from Split Rock Creek. These were kids from all over the world and many did not have their own winter gear, so they were wearing an assortment of giveaways— oversized army jackets, foam-filled Moon-Boots, and a rainbow collection of scarves and mittens, making us a colorful international group.

There was anticipation, and some anxiety, as we climbed down the bank to the cobblestone beach, where the creek emptied into a little bay. The bay was open and we stopped to talk to a man who was trying unsuccessfully to entice a fish onto his hook. Old wooden pilings jutted out of the water, and each wore a crystal collar of ice.

Mike led the way up into the woods. On the north-facing slopes the snow was knee-deep; and we struggled along, going up one hill, around boulders, and into the sunny side that faced the lake. Someone (very likely the leader) threw a snowball, and soon we had a barrage of white stuff, mixed with yelps and laughter.

We reached a promontory, and each person who climbed up to the summit turned to lend a hand to the one behind. Spread before us was the great expanse of Lake Superior, and shining in the sun to our left was the Split Rock Lighthouse. It was an exhilarating moment. The boisterousness of the earlier hike settled into a meditative silence as we all retreated inward to think about the great diversity, yet the unifying factors, in our world. Lake Superior is a good place to contemplate the world, not only because of its size, but because of its multinational-multistate shoreline and the international traffic it bears.

We all came from different backgrounds, different cultures, yet we could all appreciate the beauty of this secluded, wild place. For some of the kids, Lake Superior was a vivid reminder of the oceans near their homes. We talked about the planet, the fragility of its ecosystems, and the need for all of us to care and be active in protecting it.

We warmed ourselves on the dark rock, like lizards on a cool morning, and it was hard to leave the tranquility. Our energy returned, though, as we bounded down a snowy slope just behind a pair of white-tailed deer.

We came to the cove known as Little Two Harbors, which lies just west of the lighthouse. Here a small group of Norwegian fishermen settled and worked prior to World War I. When not fishing, they could be counted on as hired hands when extra jobs or building projects needed to be done at the lighthouse. By 1925, the fishing colony was abandoned, and the wave-washed pebbles reveal no evidence of its existence.

The lighthouse and the memories of the fishing village reminded us of a time when sailors ventured out onto the water armed only with their instincts, courage, and need for adventure. "A guiding light" and "a beacon in the night," phrases we use to describe safe passage or a way to solve a problem, are literally true of lighthouses.

Lighthouses and their keepers have developed a romantic, as well as a practical, significance to sailor and landlubber alike. Most often the image that comes to mind is a small boat tossed in storm-driven waves, the brave captain gripping the wheel, searching the

(D. Dietrich)

horizon for some sign of refuge. Then the light appears, flickering briefly as the boat crests one wave and dives into another. Safe harbor is within reach.

My illusions were somewhat shattered when I discovered that the development of lighthouses came about not because of a humanitarian concern for the safety of small fishing boats, like those that would have used this cove, but because of the concern for commerce on a large scale. The first light was built at the entrance of Boston Harbor, because of its importance as a port of call in the New World.

As the wave of exploration and expansion swept westward, the Great Lakes became important in the economy, and so in the early 1800s, lighthouses were built on Lakes Ontario and Erie. Lighthouses on Lake Superior first appeared in 1849. Six years later, the Sault Sainte Marie locks were ready for the large boats, and the floodgates released a surge of commercial shipping that continued to grow for almost a century.

A light was built on Minnesota Point, near Duluth, but it had little to do, since it was completed just after the Panic of 1857. In the 1880s, other dreamers and schemers saw the potential riches in the rocky land. Though they weren't able to secure a real lighthouse, a lantern was installed in the cupola of a private home in Beaver Bay to serve as a guiding light to the increasing ship traffic.

In 1884, the first ship left Two Harbors with a load of iron ore, and the far western shore of the great lake drew ships like a magnet, even while the iron deposits caused their compass needles to swing.

In 1885, a light was built further up the shore at Grand Marais. The original structure was replaced in 1922, but the current lighthouse still holds the original Fresnel lens.

In 1892, the Duluth harbor sent out its first load of iron ore to join the parade leaving from Two Harbors, which got its lighthouse the same year.

The Two Harbors light was the first major lighthouse structure built on the west end of the lake. It's a red-brick two-story house with a gabled roof, and the forty-nine-foot light tower is part of the house. It was the last Great Lakes lighthouse to be manned by the U.S. Coast Guard. When a terrible storm season in 1905 caused damage to thirty ships, the owners of more than five hundred freighters met and decided that what was most needed was a lighthouse with a fog signal in the vicinity of Split Rock.

Surveyor Thomas Clark described this location as "good for a lighthouse" in his 1854 mapping expedition. No one knows for sure how Split Rock came to be called such, but there is speculation that it may refer to the white streaks of anorthosite that course through the black diabase, giving the appearance of a split rock.

Navigation along the North Shore was complicated by the ore deposits that confused the early compasses. If a vessel chose to follow the coastline for guidance, it was exposed to rocky headlands and shoals, with few natural harbors for protection. The shipping companies believed a lighthouse would solve these problems.

A report written by the Eleventh District Office of the Lighthouse Board questioned the increased safety that a light would provide, because "It is a well known fact that vessels in the iron ore trade make a practice of running under virtually full speed, regardless of fog or thick weather. But for this feature of present practice, there would be no need of either a light or fog signal at or near Split Rock Point."

When we arrived at the lighthouse we took turns posing in front of it for photographs. The buildings were all closed, as they would have been in the past, when the station shut down from December to April.

We looked up at the light, and through the windows we could see the huge Fresnel lens, weighing nearly six and a half tons, that for almost six decades lit the way for countless boats, both big and small, and guided them away from the treacherous shallows along the North Shore.

If I could go back in time, to the days when Split Rock was a functioning lighthouse and an enclosed community of three families, there is one event I would most like to see. It happened in the spring when the keepers and their families came back and were getting everything out of winter storage. There are two long black foghorns that point out at the lake from the roof of the signal building. Gunny sacks would be stuffed into them in the fall to keep the snow and ice out, and removed in the spring. This is how one of the girls who grew up at the lighthouse describes the scene: "In the spring, they would start up the engines, get up pressure and blow the sacks out — shooting them out over the lake like torpedoes."

A winter fog cloaks the light at the end of the pier in Duluth Harbor. (D. Cox)

The six and one-half ton Fresnel lens remains in the light tower, where it guided sailors on the Great Lake for almost six decades. (J. and A. Mahan)

A birch forest covers a slope in Split Rock Lighthouse State Park. (M. Magnuson)

HIKING TRAILS

SUPERIOR HIKING TRAIL by Kate Crowley

The idea of hoisting a pack containing all your food and shelter, tying on sturdy hiking boots, and marching down a wooded trail, with solitude and adventure as your companions, is alluring. To start at the beginning of a trail and complete the entire route brings a great sense of accomplishment. Over the years I've read people's inspiring accounts of hiking the Appalachian Trail, and I've dreamed of doing the same thing.

The 2100-mile Appalachian Trail is fifty years old, the predecessor to the Pacific Crest Trail, the Florida Trail, the Oregon Trail, and the partially completed North Country Trail. All offer long-distance, continuously marked trails. A chance for the hiker to test body and soul, explore new territory, and traverse diverse sections of this country.

It's nice to know that now we have the opportunity to break into long-distance hiking in Minnesota with the development of the Superior Hiking Trail, which is being built on the high ridges that run parallel to the North Shore.

The Sawtooth ridges are located two to three miles inland. The highest is Eagle Mountain, which is 2301 feet above sea level (it is also the highest point in the state). Carlton Peak's summit is 924 feet above Superior's surface. The trail connects nine peaks, and they offer a good cardiovascular workout for any hiker.

In 1987, construction began on the trail with funds provided by the Legislative Commission on Minnesota Resources. The one-million-dollar project is funded by the state of Minnesota, but future maintenance costs and work are covered by the nonprofit Superior Hiking Trail Association. This group is dependent on the help and interest of private individuals, 4-H clubs, church groups, school groups, conservation clubs, and scout troops to do the maintenance work. Each group of volunteers is responsible for a five-mile section of trail.

This is the true test of the trail's value. If there are enough people who believe in it and use it, it will prosper and serve generations of hikers. If sections aren't maintained, they will return to wilderness.

* * *

We hiked our first section of the trail on a late September day with Tom Martinson, the Lake County trail coordinator. After parking just off Highway 61, Tom led us up the slope to a portion of the trail that runs between Split Rock Lighthouse and Beaver Bay. He wanted to check on some crews that were putting the finishing touches to this ten-mile stretch of trail. According to the Superior Hiking Trail Association newsletter, this section has "some of the most remote backcountry the trail has to offer."

The trail is for people on foot. Horses, trail bikes, mountain bikes, snowmobiles, and ATVs would all increase erosion of the thin-soiled trail. Managing the trail is a great challenge; as Tom emphasized, "Our plan is not to manage the land, but to manage the people using it."

The trail is narrow, averaging eighteen inches wide, and primitive, except on slopes that have carefully built steps, made of either wood block or stones, to help prevent runoff and erosion problems. Smooth lichen-covered feldspar domes jut out of the trees, providing hikers with a chance to sit and absorb the panorama while they catch their breath and ease the packs off their backs.

We went up and down several hills, and frequently were rewarded with breathtaking views of the great blue lake. The weather was fairly typical for fall along the North Shore. Thick gray clouds rolled overhead, occasionally parting long enough to shine a spotlight on the yellow aspens and birch. After scrambling for the camera and getting it focused, I'd see the gap close and the photo opportunity would be gone. Even without sunshine, there is a dramatic quality to a lead-gray sky fronted by a mix of warm reds, yellows, and orange. The contrast is so great that the colors jump out.

Tom led us down to an active beaver pond with two lodges and two dams. It is near one of the many campsites that have been built along the trail. We noticed

(R. Morreim)

that the beavers had been helping the workers by removing some of the smaller aspens along the trail. It looked like a beautiful spot to camp in the fall, but I wondered about the insect population in this thick, low woods during the summer.

The trail took us through a stand of unusually large quaking aspen and into a stand of old cedars, with their characteristically twisted trunks. One cedar had actually fallen over, and a branch had taken root and begun to develop as a new trunk. It took us several minutes of observation to see the unusual development of a tree on a tree.

We saw a ruffed grouse hurry across the trail and disappear into the brush, but the other wildlife in the vicinity left only tracks or droppings for us to identify. A moose track is easy to spot, with its big split hoof, as long as my hand, pressed deep into the soft, wet parts of the trail. Deer tracks appear delicate in comparison. Walking on tiptoe, they meander from one side of the trail to the other, looking for browse.

A black bear left its calling card, right smack in the middle of the trail—a large, dark pile of partly digested berries. Only a lucky hiker will see a wolf on the trail, but they are in the area and left telltale droppings on the trail.

This was an easy day's hike. We covered five miles in a few hours, unburdened by heavy packs—just a sampling of the entire trail's potential.

* * *

We returned a year later to hike the section above the town of Silver Bay that leads to Tettegouche State Park. On this hike we brought along Mike's mother, Alta. She enjoys daily walks of two to three miles, and we thought she was ready to graduate to some more challenging terrain. We chose the end of September again, when the fall colors would be best, the biting insects would be gone, and temperatures would be cool. Combining those advantages, this may be the best time of year for backpacking.

True to form, the sky was cloud covered and the temperatures in the fifties—perfect for comfortable hiking. The trail enters from a boulevard running up from town. A small brown sign, placed right at the edge of the woods, identifies the trail and gives the distances to Bean Lake, Bear Lake, and Tettegouche. We set Bean Lake, a walk of 2.6 miles, as our goal.

The symbol for the trail is shaped like an elm leaf and depicts green hills meeting blue water, with "Superior Hiking Trail" inscribed along the base. Little markers bearing this image are attached to trees along the route, to let you know you're headed the right way. No matter how seasoned the hiker and how spectacular the scenery, everyone needs a little boost along the way, a sign that you are on the right trail and that others have gone this far too!

Silver Bay looked clean and neatly laid out from this vantage point, but we were anxious to leave it behind. Over our shoulders, to the northwest, the hills were mottled green and yellow, with an occasional maple flaring red.

The shrub layer was full of subtle blendings of rust, purple, and scarlet. A single honeysuckle bush had a full range of autumn colors, while a Juneberry's leaves were reddish-orange, etched with veins of yellow. White and lavender asters were still in bloom, and big thimbleberry leaves still held their summer green. At the right time of year, hikers on this trail could treat themselves to a harvest of strawberries, raspberries, blueberries, or thimbleberries.

The next clearing gave us a view of the lake, and the air over the water was so clear we could easily see the outer islands of the Apostles—some fifty miles away. The air magnified a distant freighter and it appeared much closer than it actually was.

Alta kept up a good pace as we moved away from the lake view and into a stunning paper birch forest. The birch has gradually moved down from the tundra and grows in pure stands on cool, moist, wooded slopes.

Why is it that birch trees in the fall seem to stand out from everything else around them? Maybe it is their chalk-white trunks with black engravings, topped by green blending to golden-yellow leaves.

The paper birch has attracted people from the earliest times. Its bark was used by Native Americans not only to build canoes but also to construct shelters and to make containers to store or carry food.

We stood by one birch, whose old paper-thin bark was hanging in curled tendrils, exposing the newer sand-colored bark. The birch sheds its bark as it grows, much as our skin peels from sunburn. Peeling the bark away from a living tree leaves a dark ugly scar, so if you are gathering bark to build a fire, use only the pieces that can be found on fallen decaying logs—or do as most backpackers do now and carry a stove.

In a low wet area there were birds at every level and in all the trees. A pair of downy woodpeckers pounded on a dead birch tree, and golden-crowned kinglets gave their thin, high whistles as they flitted from treetop to treetop. A brown creeper circled the trunk of a spruce, and Mike spotted a solitary vireo, a Cape May warbler, and a palm warbler, all cloaked in their confusing robes of fall coloration. This was just a small sampling of the migration that occurs along the North Shore, as the birds avoid crossing the big water on their way south before winter's onslaught.

I picked up the scent of balsam poplar, the sweet perfume of the north woods. A chipmunk darted around a boulder, stared at us for a moment, and then shot across the trail and into its rocky den to await our passage.

We spooked two ruffed grouse on this hike. One burst out of hiding and squawked as it went flying through the underbrush. The other was sneaky. It saw us coming and quickly tiptoed into the shrubbery and found a good hiding spot.

Walking through a fall forest is sensory overload; blink and the stark contrast in colors seems extra-dimensional. Look down and you almost become diz-

The success of the North Shore Hiking Trail is dependent on those who use it. Various groups of volunteers maintain five-mile sections. (K. Crowley)

27

zy with the blend of yellow and brown medallions that carpet the path. It is the task of the conifer to maintain equilibrium, to hold its green and stabilize the scenery. It provides the contrast that lets autumn show off.

In the maple forest the light filtered through the thick canopy, creating a different feeling. With golden-brown leaves semicrisp underfoot, Alta said, "It gives you a warm feeling to walk through here." The decades of leaf matter had built up a spongy trail.

From another ridge we could see big slabs of dark rock, washed in earth tones, and in the valley we could see a boglike lake. Honking geese were hidden by the thick clouds. Thrush, robins, and winter wrens populated the forest.

We heard the little stream before we saw it. Set in a narrow gully, it sang a gentle siren song as it danced over rocks and sticks. The water slipped and leaped down the shiny black rocks into a narrow, deep, moss-covered grotto—a perfect hiding place for wood nymphs.

A steep series of rocks set into the hill took us up to our last ridge, where we could look back with satisfaction over the distance we had covered. The view was gorgeous, and except for the red top of a water tower and a radio tower, we could have been hundreds of miles away from civilization.

Alta had reached her limit of climbing, so she sat and soaked up the scenery while Mike and I went a little farther to the overlook on Bean Lake. Looking almost straight down, we could see the secluded lake nestled within black volcanic walls. Bean Lake sits in the basin created by two faults. The trees in the valley go right to the water's edge, and their autumn colors flow on past the horizon.

The three of us covered 5.6 miles in three and a half hours. Alta had never hiked so far in such challenging terrain, so she came away with a new sense of accomplishment. We experienced the trail's value for those seeking short day hikes with easy access to nearby resorts and communities.

The trail will cover two hundred miles when it is complete—reaching from Duluth to the Canadian border.

GEORGE CROSBY MANITOU by Mike Link

The rain was continual, five inches in a twelve-hour period, and the trails of red clay from old glacial Lake Duluth were slick. These are steep hills; clay can mold the land into steep walls and narrow grooves. This was a pottery landscape.

The vegetation was saturated, not internally but externally. The trunks of all the trees were dark with wetness, and rivulets filled the bark crevices. Leaves hung down, and the shallow valleys of veins held lilliputian lakes that coalesced at the tips and bent them earthward. Water moved from leaf to leaf, traveling a zigzag course, while water tension held droplets on each leaf tip.

The punky wood of old rotten trees acted like a sponge, and the sphagnum doubled and tripled in mass.

Brushing against the large maple-like leaf of a thimbleberry was equivalent to using a washcloth. My clothes were soaked, and water condensed between my skin and the raincoat that I tried to use for protection. Giving up, I discarded the waterproof coat and the layer of soggy clothes that clung to my skin. My backpack absorbed water from each contact it made. First it was just the pack, but then the moisture slowly moved inward until my night camp consisted of a dry sleeping bag within a thoroughly saturated tent.

I was backpacking George Crosby Manitou State Park during the rainy season—September. It had been raining for five days, so I gave in to the dampness and just had fun. Getting wet is partly a psychological proposition. Backpackers dance gingerly around puddles until they finally get their feet wet; then the trip progresses easily because the hiker can take a normal stride and look around, accepting rather than watching out for puddles.

The colored leaves of mountain and sugar maples glistened with a wet sheen, and each glacial cobble seemed freshly polished. The river collected the excess rain, gathered it from hill and tree, and confined it to a valley. I slept near a waterfall and listened as the river's increasing strength and volume grew louder. The wet tent was a barrier that let in sound and held the wetness in suspension. I slept well and enjoyed two more days of exploration.

Crosby Manitou is lightly used compared to other northern parks, so it offers a special opportunity for solitude and seclusion. There are no crowds here, and that is by design.

The park abuts the North Shore, but its entrance is inland, off back roads from Finland and Schroeder. It is just behind the wall of the Lake Superior rim, in a landscape that does not receive the moderating effect of the big lake's open winter water. This is northern border country, the kind of scenery that the canoe country lakes are known for. There are lakes with bog plants, and the northern forest dominates the park.

Bear, deer, moose, and wolf roam these woods with the backpackers. Pitcher plants, sundews, orchids, and pyrolas bloom in the summer, and a combination of hardwoods and conifers give autumnal contrast.

Crosby Manitou is often compared, sometimes disparagingly, with Isle Royale and the Superior Hiking Trail. I would not describe it as similar to Isle Royale, except that it is a remote forest-dominated system of trails. I would not describe it as similar to the Superior Hiking Trail either, because it lacks the vistas and the lake effect. It is a spot for introspection, a place to slow down and concentrate on the subtle rather than the spectacular, a place to walk rather than drive. It is a breath of remoteness preserved among the hills that surround the big lake.

28

Oberg Mountain is one of the "peaks" along the Sawtooth Range that provides the hiker with awe-inspiring panoramas.
(P. Sundberg)

The High Falls on the Baptism River is Minnesota's tallest waterfall. The water pours over the edge and churns up bushels of foam. (D. Braud)

30

RIVER MEMORIES

BY MIKE LINK

GOOSEBERRY FALLS

The North Shore collage has many features, but without the rivers tumbling and cascading down chutes of volcanic rock, it would not be the same place. Nothing else in the Midwest is as spectacular as the North Shore rivers, and I say that without qualification. There are many places of beauty, solitude, and wilderness, but when I stand deep within one of these river valleys, I feel a seclusion that carries me deep into the earth's history.

The Gooseberry River tumbles over ancient lava flows, moving toward the lake down a series of geologic steps. Each falls is a benchmark in time, an outpouring from a gigantic rift that nearly split our continent a billion years ago. The massive crack extended from northeastern Minnesota almost to Wichita, Kansas.

The earth was young then, lacking the continents that we now know, but the pressures within were creating a changes without. The supercontinents were splitting and cracking. Eventually the surface would stabilize into the current continents, but there were false starts, and this rift is the result of one near-miss that could have split North America into two continents.

Each lava flow marks a period of geologic eruption, inner disturbances that sent masses of molten material flowing to the surface. In between eruptions, the rocks were exposed to air, water, and erosion. There were periods when the rock crumbled and deposits of sandstone were left in places like Cutface Creek and Lief Erickson Park. During these periods the surfaces of old flows crumbled and decayed. The angular rock fragments were then incorporated into the bottom of the next lava sequence, creating a brecciated zone — a good benchmark for geologists who like to decipher the events of time.

As the lava erupted, large hunks were thrown into the air and came back with a splat (lava bombs), which can be found in the otherwise uniform rock tongues along the North Shore. These even retain their impact wrinkles, preserved for over a billion years.

Gases were abundant and could be explosive, but often they just drifted upward in the cooling magma and became trapped beneath the hardening surface. These bubbles created holes in the rock — vesicles — that filled with agates, Thompsonites, and other minerals as the gases cooled and minerals solidified. These vesicular zones mark the tops of the flows and give the geologist another benchmark.

In Gooseberry Park, the river has marked the flows through erosion. If you look from the bridge, a honeycomb pattern is apparent in the rocks at the top of one of the falls. The rocks along the river's edge show the same distinct angles and straight sides. This is a pattern of cooling that volcanic rocks have. They shrink and solidify, isolating large volcanic columns.

When the flow is intact, the columns stand for billions of years and the cracks seem minor. But when the columns are exposed, water can seep between them. Unlike lava, water expands when it freezes, and frost wedges the columns apart.

Of all the North Shore rivers, Gooseberry shows the most human-caused erosion. It is too accessible, too visited, too trammeled. I visit it in off-seasons, when the snow buries the effects of too many footsteps, when the parking lot does not resemble a shopping center and the voices of mildly interested visitors don't drown out the spirit voices of the tumbling water.

Gooseberry is the most obvious of our North Shore rivers. A waterfall to the north of the highway tumbles in the peripheral vision of each driver who passes over the bridge, and a canyon falls away to the south. The road may give passersby a glimpse at the beauty, but it creates a scar. These falls can never be wild again — the wildness has been stolen by the engineers and planners. I hate the bridge and its placement, but I am still caught up by the view that it offers.

BAPTISM RIVER

The Baptism River is completely different from the Gooseberry. Its rocks are darker and its canyon seems more remote, although I fear the impact of the newly

31

With ice hammer and crampons, a climber scales a frozen waterfall. (B. Firth)

expanded Tettegouche State Park. I have walked and skied up and down this canyon to the High Falls. From the lake, it is a dancing waterway, with currents moving from side to side, around dark boulders, curling in frothy eddies and souse holes.

In the winter, I have crossed thin ice bridges and skied down the waterfalls beneath High Falls. Then it is a white wilderness with tracks of deer and otter, mink and marten. There are places where the deer drinks the cool river water, places where turbulence and snow conditions prevent the river from freezing solid.

Waterfalls flow behind ice curtains, and ice forms in a variety of colors, depending on the temperature, the speed of freezing, and the frothiness of the water itself. The ice clings to the river's edge, piles up beneath the falls, and forms icicles in hidden recesses. As the win-

ter progresses, the spray adds layers to the ice formations, and then it is redirected as it hits its own creations. The waterfall freezes not in a single blanket, but as a sculpture garden—frozen energy in a three-dimensional cocoon.

Ice hammer and crampons are the only ways to traverse the frozen falls. They bite into the ice and emphasize the variations. Some ice shatters, some sucks the ice axe in and won't let go. Brittle, soft blue, black, white. The waterfall is as distinct in winter as in summer. Each person who ventures to the falls with respect and time comes away with a different perspective.

My son, Matthew, is one of the rare breed of individuals who see the North Shore streams as boating rivers. He pictures himself shooting down the white water and slaloming among the rocks. His is a per-

Only an expert can encounter the power and beauty of a North Shore river. (B. Firth)

spective that few people can know. He interacts with the river in a kayak, a small piece of plastic and fiberglass with barely enough interior to accept his lower body. He describes his run down the Baptism:

"The North Shore streams are more intimate than other northern rivers, more enclosed in tight canyons. The sounds reverberate off the canyon walls and everything seems closer here.

"There is more of a sense of falling than floating. It is a sense of speed rather than power. Everything is tight and technical, with precise movements and perfect timing required. It is tough to see what is ahead, because the rivers are constantly going around bends or over horizon lines. All of a sudden you are there, and it drops off ten to fifteen feet, at thirty-five miles per hour or more."

The kayak can do amazing things, but only if the paddler gives it the proper commands, executes the proper moves, and anticipates. It is an extension of the paddler, not a separate vehicle. The kayak can roll over, but the paddler can bring it back up again almost instantly. The kayak can surf and dance on its end, but only if the paddler has the balance and confidence that requires.

In a kayak, you must go faster or slower than the current, you must have confidence and skill, especially on this river. "There are three unrunable drops on the Baptism at any water level. You have to make the eddy and get out just above each. You feel more isolated. It's a long way out."

Two Step is not unrunable, nor is the plunge just above it. "The adrenaline is just pumping. It's a rush."

When the ice comes out, it's a rush the other way. The fishermen line the shores for steelhead, waders

For the fisherman, North Shore rivers mean the possibility of trout or salmon on the line. (P. Sundberg)

make everyone waddle, and the shorelines are a maze of skinny wands and translucent threads. Salmon eggs, spinners, hooks, spoons. Each person maneuvers for the space that will let him or her put a monofilament into the right fishing hole.

They are after rainbow trout; *steelhead* is the name of the variety, not the species. Planted in the lake as far back as 1895, steelhead have been able to survive in a wide variety of habitats. They spawn up streams like their relative the coho, but they do not die after spawning as the salmon do. Their upstream adventure includes fighting currents of meltwater in engorged rivers, jumping and dancing in the frothy waters of cascades and waterfalls, and emerging from the spray in leaps of prodigious heights and distance. When they reach the proper gravel bed, they release spawn and sperm to produce the next generation.

The adults then weave a pattern between the lures, riding the current like submerged kayakers, and end up back in the lake. The spawn will remain in the streams for as long as fourteen months, then migrate to the open waters of the lake. It is difficult to imagine how these animals can adjust from the stream to the parameters of the great lake. Lake Superior fish have been found as far away as Lakes Michigan and Huron.

On shore, the annual migration of two-legged casters can be a comedy of twisted lines as fisherman catches fisherman, waders become wading pools, and debates arise over temporary ownership of various shoreline rocks. The purpose is to land a gleaming steelhead with its colorful array of stripes, to watch the sun glisten on its shiny scales, to feel the fight and strength of the catch, and ultimately to eat the cold, firm flesh of the trout.

It is also a time to watch the dislodging of small icebergs that teeter on the brink of the falls, to feel the spray as the ice plummets from the lip to the pool, and to hear the grating of ice on ice, the song of breakup.

The Baptism has Minnesota's tallest waterfall, but that has little real meaning. It is a statistic in a realm of emotion. The height does not matter, the effect does: the large reflective pool beneath the imposing cliff, the rainbow rising like a spawning trout in the sunlight of summer, the deer moving out from one forest edge and gingerly walking across the falls and into the next patch of woods. This is a picture of reddish rocks, green forests, blue skies, and root-beer-colored waters. It is sound, coolness, wet spray, warm sun, cool breeze, and remnant ice patches in the lushness of summer.

CARIBOU RIVER

The Caribou River always looks so mild in comparison to the other streams along the North Shore. Where the road passes over it, the stream washes gravel like the braided streams in Alaska. It comes out of a large valley, but there is no rock showing—only

glacial materials and a parking lot. But I have many memories from this river.

Perhaps the most lasting impression comes from a woman who was on a trip with one of the naturalists at Northwoods Audubon Center. It might have been the subtleness of the trailhead as much as the muddiness of the trail, but this traveler from Big Canoe, Georgia, was not excited about walking a mile to see the falls, especially if it meant getting her feet wet. Craig pleaded with her, tried to entice her to give it a try, knowing that the reward would justify the wet feet, but she stopped, looked him in the eyes, and said, "No, I've already seen a waterfalls. They're all alike."

The glacial clays and gravels give way to the bedrock right at the falls, and it is spectacular. A small river, confined to a faultbound canyon far above the lake, is suddenly released where its energies can erode the easily moved glacial materials. Here the valley floor drops suddenly, and the river makes the adjustment

Lower Manitou Falls. (D. Dietrich)

Like all the rivers of the North Shore, the Temperance ends its journey by mixing waters with cold Lake Superior. (M. Magnuson)

from suspended valley to road level in one great leap into a box canyon that makes a right turn from the upper valley. Steep walls surround it, and a circular pool lies below the plunge.

In the winter, the falls has a long sloping apron of ice that reaches from canyon to pool. I have always found this to be an intriguing formation and could not resist climbing it on one winter trip. The climb was strenuous but not particularly tough. I relied on my ice ax, but it was not a sheer vertical face of ice. It was a challenge and it was fun.

However, my bad back decided to demonstrate why I have given up climbing; as soon as I reached the top and safety, it went into a spasm that sent me crashing into the snow.

I was no longer having fun. My muscles were in a tight knot and I could not look out across the valley toward the lake and appreciate the scene that unfolded before me. Just then a Japanese student who had walked up, rather than taking my ice route, appeared. He looked at me and paused, unable to comprehend why I was lying there, not knowing how to communicate what he wanted to in English nor quite grasping what I was telling him. Finally, in awkward confusion he looked up, then back down to me. "This is a beautiful place. We do not have anything like this in Japan." I agreed with him.

CUTFACE CREEK

What a name! I enjoy this creek for its contrast with the other North Shore rivers. Here the bedrock that dominates the lower valley is sandstone, rather than volcanic rock. It is erosional debris from one of the calm periods between volcanic activities. I walk upstream past the wire mesh erosion-and-stream-stabilization structures that line the river, and enjoy the sweeping vista of sandstone that was first laid down by rivers, and then cut by one. It is a story of thin beds, crossbeds, and ripplemarks, of sandstone overlaying lava and overlain by lava—a scene from another landscape, and a time-lapse study of the present one.

The lava near the creek is best know for its Thompsonite beach, with rocks like bloodshot eyes. Thompsonite, a semiprecious stone that is abundant in this small area, forms in some lava vesicles. It is a soft zeolite mineral formation that must be removed from much harder rock to be valuable. It comes in shades of cream, pink, and orange-red.

Thompsonite is not found at the mouth of the creek, although some agates are. The stream enters a big harborlike beach, with a reef of rocks a half mile or more out into the lake. Above it, the road swings around the lava before dipping down into the valley that was carved in the softer sandstone. It was from this vantage point on one trip that I could see an animal swimming out toward the rocks—a fairly large mammal that seemed intent on "going out to sea." I was with two others and we had a canoe on the vehicle, so we put it in and paddled out onto the glassy waters of the bay to investigate.

You experience a sense of humbleness when you take a canoe onto Lake Superior. I am used to sailing the lake on bigger vessels, and the canoe just doesn't feel like it can handle the quick mood changes of Superior, so I paddle on the big waters with much more concern than on white-water rivers.

The rocks are not covered with algae, and the water is so clear that the rocks always appear closer than they really are. It is a deceptive quality that lures boats out farther than they should go. On this paddle it didn't matter, because the lake remained somnolent.

As the canoe pushed through the water, the head of the animal took on a smaller size than I expected. From the shore, I thought it looked mooselike, but as we approached we found a deer southbound to big trouble.

We paddled around the deer, herding it toward the shore. It was slow and took some encouragement to go that way, but eventually, it got to the rocks and tried to scramble up. The cold of the lake had numbed its legs and it stumbled onto the rocks, where it lay panting while we paddled away. When we returned from our hike, it was gone; only a wispy patch of wetness remained as a clue to what had taken place.

TEMPERANCE AND BRULE RIVERS

When I think of paddling, my thoughts usually turn inland to the Boundary Waters Canoe Area Wilderness and the lakes and portages that make up its countless routes. The BWCA is also the source of two of the North Shore's most beautiful rivers, the Temperance and the Brule. Both of them exit Brule Lake, and each takes a wilderness route through forest and basalt to reach Lake Superior. The Brule runs through Judge C. R. Magney State Park, and the Temperance River has a park named after it. Both rivers qualify for the National Wild River System but are not in it.

The Temperance is the cauldron river. The narrow defile, with cascades and small falls, confines the river to a frothy rivulet only three to four feet wide in parts. Trails that are swept bare of vegetation allow hikers to glimpse the turbulence. Most people keep their feet well back from the edge and peer over the rocks as though the river had a suction that would pull them in—a feeling that has some roots in all of us.

Rivers hypnotize and tantalize. They swirl and flow in gentle motions that can erupt in startling violence. They lull and lure use, then take our breath in plunges and whirlpools. The Temperance is our northern Gooseberry, another river that is spectacular but too accessible. Feet have destroyed vegetation and worn paths in the rock, and the highway bridge detracts from the wild beauty.

The entire North Shore has this same problem, the allure and the sensitivities. How do we enjoy without trampling, how do we preserve the intangibles of wild waters—lakes and rivers? How do we watch for the lichen beneath our feet when our minds are engaged in travel with the current?

The Palisades have been a source of awe and challenge since humans first encountered them. Early native people tried to shoot arrows to the top. Today, rock climbers scale and rappel down the granite walls. (J. and A. Mahan)

CLIFFS

THE MISSING ELEMENT by Kate Crowley

They said it couldn't be done, they said that the peregrine falcon was on its way to extinction and it was just too expensive, too difficult, and too complex to save it. We would have to stand by helplessly and watch it disappear. Such was the scientific opinion in the early 1970s. The peregrine had been severely affected by the pesticide DDT, and its numbers decreased worldwide throughout the 1950s and 1960s until it was no longer able to reproduce and reestablish itself in the wild.

Because the peregrine is a dramatically beautiful and athletic bird, it has historically been a favorite among falconers—those people who hunt with birds of prey, rather than weapons. A small group of concerned and stubborn falconers and scientists gathered in 1972 at Cornell University to pool their knowledge and energy in a project that would attempt to pull the bird back from the brink of oblivion.

Gradually, after researchers learned how to successfully artificially inseminate captive birds and how to hack (reintroduce to the wild) the fledglings, the East Coast began to see positive results. Soon the people at Cornell were sending young birds to other parts of the country to be used in breeding programs.

In 1982, the Minnesota Peregrine Project began, with funds from the DNR nongame program. Through the cooperative efforts of the Minnesota Raptor Research and Rehabilitation Clinic, the Bell Museum of Natural History, the Nature Conservancy, the U.S. Fish and Wildlife Service, the Forest Service, and private falconers, a plan to bring the peregrines back to Minnesota was developed.

The first releases occurred along the bluffs of the Mississippi River in southern Minnesota. There was success, but there was also disappointing failure. Great horned owls preyed on the parentless falcons, and fledglings met with disaster on nearby highways and train tracks.

It was time to look for other sites in the state. Peregrines once nested on Shovel Point on the North Shore, so in March 1984 the concerned agencies and individuals met in Tofte to consider the possibilities.

Steve Hoecker, a wildlife biologist for the Forest Service at the time, remembers going out to check three possible sites. "It was still the middle of winter and we had to go in on snowshoes. We checked the palisades on Clearwater Lake off the Gunflint Trail, South Fowl Lake on the Arrowhead Trail, and Leveaux Mountain, which is in the Tofte district. All three were good sites for the peregrines, but we settled on Leveaux because it had good access for the people who would be doing the preparatory work and release.

"The site was about a mile from the road and up a pretty steep climb. We had to make a trail into it and set up a base camp. I remember the blackflies were really bad, but it was ready by the end of June and around the fourth of July we released the five birds."

The major source of funds for this release was private donations to the Nature Conservancy, with some DNR nongame funds and staff assistance from the Forest Service. The cost of the birds alone was close to two thousand dollars apiece.

In addition to the five released in 1984, ten birds were released in 1985, and eighteen in 1986. Because of the limited locations appropriate for release, people working on the program tried some new approaches. According to Wayne Russ, another Forest Service employee in the Tofte district, "We sort of added a new twist to release science. We released three batches out of one box. It was hectic, because you had some of the older birds flying around and harassing the younger fledglings, but not to the total detriment of the plan. It worked. We also took a bird from one release site and put it at another, which hadn't been tried before."

In the two years since the last birds were released along the North Shore, some encouraging and exciting things have happened. A courting pair was seen near Leveaux Mountain. It is believed that the male generally returns to the site first and waits to call in a passing female. When he sights one, he calls out "*wichew*" and flies out from his perch to get her attention. If he is successful, the ensuing courtship flights are stunning.

Joseph A. Hagar, a Massachussetts ornithologist, gives a colorful account of one such flight he observed in the mid-1930s: "Again and again the tercel [male falcon] started well to leeward and came along the cliff against the wind, diving, plunging, saw-toothing, rolling over and over, darting hither and yon, like an autumn leaf until finally he would swoop up into the full current of air and be borne off on the gale to do it all over again. At length, he tired of this, and, soaring in narrow circles without any movement of his wings other than a constant adjustment of their planes, he rose to a position 500 or 600 feet above the mountain and north of the cliff. Nosing over suddenly, he flicked his wings rapidly 15 to 20 times and fell like a thunderbolt. Wings half closed now, he shot down past the north end of the cliff, described three successive vertical loop-the-loops across its face, turning completely upside down at the top of each loop, and roared out over our heads with the wind rushing through his wings like ripping canvas. . . . We felt a strong impulse to stand and cheer."

Just as exciting was the successful nesting of a pair of peregrines on Palisade Head in 1988. This is a popular cliff for rock climbers, and it was some unsuspecting climbers who learned they were near the nest when the parents suddenly flew out, dove, and loudly cried, "*cack, cack, cack,*" at the intruders. Two young hatched from this nest. The parents were a male from the Tofte release and a female from a release in downtown Minneapolis.

Peregrine is derived from the Latin *peregrinus*, which means "a wanderer," so it was not surprising to find the female some three hundred miles north of her release site. Other banded birds have made their way from Red Wing, Minnesota, to New Jersey and from Rochester, Minnesota, to Milwaukee, Wisconsin.

With these successes, the peregrine people are cautiously optimistic about the future. It has been rewarding to see the interest the public has shown in the project. Steve Hoecker was somewhat surprised, but pleased, with the public response. He says, "It was neat to see the level of enthusiasm along the shore, from the resort owners to the tourist coming up. They all wanted to know more about peregrines. In that first summer we must have done over 250 programs on the birds, at different locations. I was getting all kinds of letters and calls, including letters from school kids in Ohio."

But what really struck him and said the most about the whole purpose of the reintroduction was a conversation with the man whose land the release took place on. He had been coming up to his cabin since he was a boy. The summer they released the birds, he suddenly knew what had been missing from this striking wild landscape. It had been years since he had heard the screaming calls of young peregrines, who chase one another in fledgling play. As soon as he heard them, the memories came flooding back and he knew what an emptiness their absence had created.

THE LANDSCAPE by Mike Link

My rope is secure on a tree that is a hundred years old, with roots anchored in the Precambrian. As I back to the edge of the escarpment, the line between me and the tree still has some slack in it, and my waist jingles with carabiners and a figure-eight loop that connect my harness with my lifeline. It is a strange sensation, backing up to and over a cliff. It is an act of faith in equipment and technique to go over the edge and into space.

The cliff feels secure and permanent, but looking over my shoulder I can see rocks splitting the incoming waves into spray and surf a hundred feet below, rocks that were once part of this cliff. There is the moment of commitment and I go. Soon the equilibrium of my world is shifted. I feel rocks against my feet, but the force of gravity does not hold me to the cliff. I feel comfortable, yet almost giddy. I bound off the rock, slip rope through the figure-eight loop, and come back to the cliff. Soon the cliff face becomes undercut and beyond the lay of my climbing rope. This is free rappelling, dancing in the wind, suspended in the air by a fiber lifeline. It is a good time to reflect on what is around me.

This cliff is one of Minnesota's best climbing walls. It is a palisade that rises from the waters as a solid monolith. Indians were impressed by this rock and shot arrows from their canoes, trying to place them on the top. I doubt if this was a process of religious significance, but rather a challenge to the Indians' shooting prowess, because of the cliff's height.

The rock is no less impressive as I dangle here. It is a rhyolite flow, a purplish rock that is lighter in weight than the dark basalt flows that dominate the shore (although picking up a rhyolite boulder does not seem any easier to me). Rhyolite is the ash, the foam on top of the volcanic brew. Its most common form is granite, the major building block of continents. Granite is the "plutonic" form of this mineral soup, the form that hardens below the surface in a steady, slow-cooling, mineral-growing environment.

When I look to the north, I see Shovel Point, another rhyolite structure, part of the same flow sequence, and I know that its purple rock mass is exposed along the road in a spectacular color display just before the Highway 1 junction. The palisade rock is columnar, like the flows at Gooseberry State Park.

This shoreline has a variety of faces. Since its ancient volcanic beginnings, these rocks have been exposed to a billion years of water, freezing, glaciers, waves, and mineral disintegration. It has changed suddenly in columnar collapse, and gradually in the dissolving of minerals through acid rain and oxidation.

To a geologist, this is a wave-cut cliff, or scarp. Shovel Point and Silver Cliffs are two more that were formed by the present lake level. East of Grand Marais there are additional scarps that are higher than the present lake. These are remnants of the erosion that took place after the glacier (10,000 years ago) and before the present Lake Superior (about 4,000 years ago), during the Nipissing Lake level.

There are islands near the shore too, archipelagoes like the Susie Islands and the cluster at the mouth of Thunder Bay's harbor, and single islands like Knife, Encampment, Five Mile, and Grand Portage. In all, there are hundreds of islands in Lake Superior. Each one represents a more resistant part of the shore, and each one is an island because of the present lake level. If the water level were to rise they would be underwater shoals, and if the level were to drop they would be hills like Palisade Head. This is differential erosion, the uneven influence of mineral distribution and the factors of erosion, like cracks and water flow.

Sometimes the islands represent other images to us. Knife Island, near Knife River, has been the sight of at least one shipwreck, and it might be the location for one of the most famous "went missing" vessels in the lake's history. The *Benjamin Noble* and the *Lambert* were within sight of one another as they cruised along the North Shore on their way to Duluth during an April 1914 nor'easter. The *Lambert* made the harbor and expected the *Noble* to be about a half hour behind. The *Benjamin Noble* never made it, although flotsam bearing her name did wash up on the Duluth shore.

No one is sure if Knife Island is the site of the wreck, but some of the lake's leading authorities believe the evidence points to this offshore island and shoal. Since navigational charts didn't even include this island and many other shoals until the 1960s, it's not hard to believe that the voyage of a ship under a 31-year-old master on his first command, in seas that inundated the lighthouses at Duluth, could end in tragedy.

The thirteen Susie Islands are folded parts of the bedrock and were connected to the mainland during the early stages of glacial melt. The glacial ice cooled the climate and the entire landscape was populated with tundra plants. Then the waters rose and inundated the land, separating some of the high spots, such as these islands.

Most North Shore islands are too small to maintain their mainland plant life or are large enough to develop a complex forest ecology, like Isle Royale. But the Susie Islands are far enough offshore to discourage invaders, and they are small enough to be bathed completely in the cold fogs of Superior. The result is a nature preserve that includes plants that grow on the permafrost of the Arctic Circle: arctic onion, northern eyebright, alpine bistort, and Norwegian witlow grass. There are also two lichens here that grow nowhere else in the state.

Sphagnum, the thick mosslike plant that dominates the northern bogs, also dominates the islands. It may have started in the small rocky depressions, which would have collected standing water, but it was taken advantage of the fogs and its own ability to absorb moisture, so that it now forms the island's carpet, over three feet deep in some places.

The sphagnum further controls the island ecology because it secretes acid in quantities that prohibit the growth of many plants. The result is a vegetative community of leatherleaf, Labrador tea, cranberry, and other bog regulars, with an overstory of black spruce and a mix of plants that would not normally be associated with a Minnesota bog complex.

Unlike the BWCAW plant communities, fire has not been a factor here, unless you talk about its absence. The moist air and carpet have kept this a nonfire ecology.

Around the sphagnum carpet are rocky shores. In addition to the two lichens, there are butterworts and round-leaved sundew, both of which entice insects to visit, then trap them and ingest the nitrogen from the carcasses.

The shoreline rockworks include much more than islands and cliffs; there are also sea caves and stone arches. Shovel Point has both, one on each side of the point. The most spectacular might be the least visible. The sea cave is a large cavity in the bedrock across a little bay on the north side (it is most visible from the highway). It is an indentation created by wave action, a sculpting of solid rock. On the south shore, the Apostle Islands boast of spectacular sea caves, but those are in sandstone, which is easily eroded. This one is a monument to the lake's energy and the persistent force of the waves.

* * *

Suspended here where peregrines fly, I let my mind drift through time changes — Archean eon to Quaternary period — from geologic, to historic, to ecological. Aren't they all connected? I can let my eyes focus on amygdules (mineral-filled cavities) in the rock beside me, or peer into the distance and be swept along with the waves. The peninsulas and bays vary from the high cliffs and hills of Canada to the low-elevation rock toes that slip into the water near Duluth. The shore is black slate in Canada and black gabbros in Duluth. There are red clays and reddish glacial moraines between and on the bedrock.

I lower myself to the cobblestone and boulder beach beneath the cliff. It feels strange at first to settle onto solid ground, to take a vertical instead of horizontal viewpoint.

I am firmly in the present, but the present is changing rapidly; the cobbles roll beneath my feet, the waves send shudders through the entire network of rocks.

There is a sample here of all the rocks of the North Shore. There is glacial erosion and shaping, which has been intensified by the lake. Moraines mark the edges of ice advance, gravel beds mark the shorelines of ancient lake levels. Old stream channels have been partially filled by younger, less energized streams. There are old deltas, modern beaches, abandoned shorelines, and stream-eroded valleys. Geologists will never run out of terms for the intrusions, extrusions, plutons, outwash plains, grabens, faults, pipes, sills, and dikes.

I stand on a rich, almost virgin landscape, freshly washed by the lake, occasionally added to by the weak parts of the cliff above. It appears lifeless, until I take

A young peregrine spreads its wings and tail in preparation for flight. (D. Cox)

my time and bend down to observe it.

On these beaches, animals precede plants in colonization. Spiders wander on the rocks scavenging, instead of weaving webs. One species of ant combs the rocks looking for dead caddis flies that have emerged from the shallows and the streams. A species of fly — genus *Hydrophorus* — is common on rocks that are constantly washed by the waves, but is seldom found on dry rocks. Ladybugs congregate on driftwood in the fall. Gulls scavenge for carrion on the rocks and add their guano to enrich the life zone.

The rock ledges are first covered by lichens and one species of moss. There are special plants on the rocky slopes, like ninebark, three-leafed cinquefoil, shrubby cinquefoil, harebell, bird's-foot primrose, and butterwort. Nothing is barren for long; the landscape is constantly changing because nature is the supreme landscape designer.

I am witness to the constancy of our planet. Where water meets land is a place of consant flux, but is it any different on the land or in the water? The peregrines on land were removed from the North Shore by human pollution and destruction; now they return because the humans have reintroduced them to the cliffs. The trout in the lake were nearly destroyed by overfishing and the unintentional introduction of sea lamprey by humans; now trout prosper by reintroduction and the management of the lamprey by humans.

We are the constant element of risk, the meddler. We toy with coastal zoning, but fail to really implement it. We dump tailings rich in asbestos into the lake, yet we can contemplate the richness of its beauty as I am doing now. And we can also understand the complexities better than any other organism on earth.

Hopes run high for the future of these imperiled falcons every time a new group is released. (D. Cox)

A hack site on the North Shore is located on a high ridge to give the young peregrines privacy and the best opportunities for success. (D. Cox)

A cobblestone beach is washed by the spray of a breaker. Waves constantly roll in and out, polishing and grinding the rocks into their distinctive oblong shapes. (B. Firth)

COBBLESTONE BEACHES

BY MIKE LINK

Cobblestones, oval rocks that cobblers might have used to shape shoes, are stacked in crescent-shaped beaches between Grand Marais and Grand Portage. The beaches are ridges of waterworn rocks, reddish in color and stacked steep by the wind and wave-driven ice. The rocks are brick-sized, some fireplace-sized, remnants of both the bedrock and the glaciers.

These crescent bays are close to the road and inviting to walk. The rocks twist and squeak beneath the feet, and walking is contorted by the movement. In the sunshine, the rocks glisten where the waves wash in and out. In the fog, they seem to sweep into oblivion. There are almost always skipping stones among the large rocks, but even the most avid skipper won't make a dent in the building forces of the lake.

Energy is cycled in many ways on earth. Now the frozen lava is tumbled landward by incoming waves and rolled back by the return surge. Since there is more energy coming in than going back, the rocks are arranged and rearranged into bands of different sizes. The larger ones tend to be both in the water and farthest up the beach.

Storms are the reason. Storms brew up great wave strength, which moves the rocks inland, but the returning wave can't move them back. Later, ice moved inland by waves stacks the pile up.

The rocks near shore may be moved gradually shoreward by ice dragging on the bottom as it moves. They eventually join the pile. In between the large cobblestones are slightly smaller stones, those that normal wave action can push partway up the beach and those that the return waves wash partway back from the storm debris.

The largest zone is the gravel area, the place where incoming and outgoing waters wash back and forth, leaving small polished souvenirs.

There are many variations to this: rocks that are heavier than other rocks of the same size, places where bedrock extends steeply into the water, and ice-stacked ridges that collapse under the force of gravity.

But walking the beach is not an act of geologic investigation, it is a romp, a clattering run, a skipping contest, a sunny stroll.

The beaches in this area differ from the shoreline in other locations. In the fog of later winter, the beach north of Colville is gray, and depth perception is erased. The bay is filled with rock reefs, some of which hold on to their ice caps. The rocks stick out of the water in deep black ridges that look like a pod of whales.

Beaches are places to stretch the imagination.

MUSHING ON THE SAWBILL

BY KATE CROWLEY

The temperature was well below zero and the sky was gray as Mike and I drove north toward the Sawbill Trail. It was mid-January and the lake was beginning to freeze near Duluth, but farther up the shore, the water was still open. A misty vapor rose and drifted over the dark gray water. The wind was blowing, but the waves were not capped; rather, they looked rounded, and the overall impression was that the water was thickened, like syrup. Not ready to freeze up yet, but not quite as fluid as a week before. Bays grabbed our attention as we whisked by, the rocks coated with ice and the water splashing against them.

We were on our way to the Sawbill checkpoint on the John Beargrease Dogsled Race. Held in January, the race honors the memory of an Ojibwa man who delivered the mail by dogsled between Two Harbors and Grand Marais during the last decade of the nineteenth century. The trails were not groomed for him, and his annual salary was far less than the purse for the first-place winner.

We listened to the radio on the way and heard an interview with a woman "musher" (the term given to those hardy people who ride or run along the back of the sled and control the dogs) who was leading the race on this, the second day.

The severe cold of the night before (thirty-five degrees below zero) had been very hard on the teams. Two competitors had already dropped out. One man came up to a judge at a checkpoint, shook him awake and handed him his bib, saying, "Here—I've had enough of this." Later, a young woman musher in her first Beargrease came in and showed the judge her hands. Two fingers and a thumb were starting to turn black with frostbite. She had to drop out of the race.

The Sawbill Trail is a narrow road that goes inland from Tofte. We arrived at the checkpoint area around 10:30 A.M., and already cars lined one side of the road. A man stopped us, and when we told him we were volunteers, he directed us up the road to park and told us where the mess tent could be found. The Beargrease is largely staffed by volunteer labor, and despite the surprises awaiting us, it runs remarkably well.

We located the small white trailer and introduced ourselves to a few men who were standing around the doorway. The working conditions weren't exactly as we'd been told they'd be. There was no electrical hookup, no light or space heater. What we had was a two-burner propane stove to cook beans, brats, and coffee on. The brats were frozen solid and being kept "cold" in a cooler. There were four cans of beans and a box of frozen buns, but no can opener, or knife, or plates. We were told someone had gone to town for supplies.

This race was running an hour slower than the year before because of the snow and temperature conditions, so business at the cookshack was slow to begin with. The trailer was located in a clearing that included a lean-to, a campfire, and a dark green tent set up for the mushers to sleep in. A van and small trailer housed the ham radio operators.

Predicting times in a dogsled race is imprecise at best. Between checkpoints, racers are seen only when they cross a roadway, and during the race they lose the trail or stop to rest their dogs or check their dogs' feet.

Rumors began to drift in that the first team was expected, so Mike sent me up to the official checkpoint with the camera. I stood near the judges, while the spectators crowded behind the plastic rope behind me. We all waited. And waited. And waited some more.

The boredom of waiting was broken by the antics of a least weasel. It was on the bridge when some people spotted it. A sleek white coat served as camouflage, but its black BB-like eyes, nose, and tail tip gave away its presence. It would tunnel into the snow and then poke its head up and stare brazenly at us. I moved down closer and watched it cross the bridge and run along the other side towards us, stopping frequently to pop up and look around. Now I know where the children's song "Pop Goes the Weasel" comes from. It poked its head up one last time near the end of the bridge, not five feet away from me, then dove down the embankment and into the woods. If I were to give it human reactions, I'd say it looked surprised by all the commotion on such a cold winter's day.

With the distraction of the weasel gone, I noticed

A musher and his team race against time and the elements. (S. Kuchera)

47

At the Sawtooth checkpoint, a team of dogs is bedded down and covered with blankets to help them rest and recharge for the next leg of the race. (M. Link)

my aching feet and began walking in place, trying to get the circulation going. It was a losing battle. When the snow began to fall and the camera started to turn white, I decided it was time to return to the trailer. Mike was handling the food line easily by himself, so I went to the fire to warm my toes.

An assistant judge for the race was sitting on a log before the fire and I asked him about the weather conditions. He said, "Highway 2 was a zoo last night. There were lots of snarls in the lines, and the snow in this cold is like ground glass on dogs' feet."

We heard a rising of voices and knew the first team was on its way in. Mike ran down to the river and saw them cross the bridge, but by the time I got my camera out of the trailer and ran to the checkpoint, the team had stopped. It was Jamie Nelson, the musher we'd heard on the radio earlier. Her dogs were panting and still straining at the harnesses.

They recorded her official time and sent her toward our area with her sled and dogs. Lots of friends and followers trailed behind, taking pictures and crowding around the dogs. I heard her say to someone, "It's hard out there." She was wearing a brown snowsuit and parka with only her eyes, nose, and mouth exposed to the air.

Each team has a group of "handlers" — people who volunteer their time and stamina to perform the necessary tasks at each checkpoint. This gives the musher as much time as possible to rest up and prepare for the next leg of the race. Handlers feed and bed down the dogs and discuss the conditions of the team with the musher. They also load everything up and drive to the next checkpoint to wait to perform their duties all over again. Sleep is not guaranteed. It's not a glamorous or high-profile job, but it is essential to the success of a team.

At Jamie's rest area, straw was brought out and spread on the ground. The dogs pawed and nosed in it, circling around as best they could, to get comfortable. Paws were checked and then food was dished out. It looked like a mixture of canned dog food and beef stew.

I was surprised by the appearance of the dogs — they were no bigger than our small female husky, and they looked pretty skinny. Jamie Nelson describes hers as "sort of a Heinz 57," but she has a strong preference for the trainability of German shepherds and likes to have that breed well represented in the mix.

Some of the resting dogs wore "booties," lightweight colored pieces of fabric that go over the paw and are secured with Velcro at the wrist. Some dogs were lying down and chewing at the ice on their paws, but one yellow dog wasn't ready to quit. It stood and leaned forward, running in place and looking around like "What's the matter with you guys, let's get going." They finally had to unharness the dog and take it to another spot to sleep alone.

Snow continued to fall, and after an hour or so, the dogs were blending into the surrounding snowbanks. People continued to walk by and look, but the handlers stood guard so that no one bothered the dogs while they slept.

The second team arrived about fifteen minutes later. This team had more Siberian huskies in it, many of them white dogs. They parked in front of Jamie's team and bedded down like the others. Handlers went from dog to dog, checking paws and applying salve where needed.

The second musher, Brad Pozarnsky, when interviewed by a news team, described the snow as "little icicles." Hard on the dogs, no matter how you describe it. Brad was a cheerful man, wearing a big parka. A beard protected most of his face, but pink cheeks and bright eyes glowed in the cold air. He said his feet had been cold all night too. At the end of the race he received the Sportsmanship Award, by popular vote from the other mushers.

The third team, run by the previous year's winner, Robin Jacobsen, arrived and whooshed back to the area by the mess tent. They parked themselves deeper in the woods and were less disturbed by onlookers. His dogs had bright-colored blankets placed over them as they slept in the falling snow.

The race is a big investment for these people. Entry fee alone is four hundred dollars, and then there are all the costs of getting to the course, coordinating a team of helpers, and all the gear, food, and transportation for the dogs. The mushers who came through Sawbill all expressed relief that they'd made it this far.

By 4:00 P.M., the first team was preparing to leave after a three-hour layover. Dogs were rousted out of sleep and somewhat grudgingly went back on the line. People gathered round to watch Jamie take off in the dusk. Television cameramen jockeyed for position along the trail, and as the team went past, a small round of applause and cheers sent them on their way. The next stretch of trail was forty-one miles long and full of steep climbs and runs. It's hard to imagine how they do it in the darkness.

As the dark began to settle in, more teams arrived at the checkpoint. We fed them hot bratwurst and beans and talked to them as they sat on the "stoop" of the trailer. Around the glowing campfire, a small circle of people clustered together, talking and trying to stay warm. Around 6:00 P.M., we finished our duty and turned our post over to another person. As we headed back to the car, we passed resting teams and mushers talking quietly to their handlers. On the road, more teams were being bedded down by their trucks, and still the snow fell.

For seven hours, we'd experienced a little of the excitement and drama that is the essence of dogsled racing. It's fun to imagine yourself out there with the dogs, racing against time and the elements and the sleds coming up behind. But it's a hard sport and one that most of us would prefer to watch from the sidelines, to admire the animals and the people who challenge themselves in the winter wilderness.

* * *

Sunday night, really Monday morning — 12:30 A.M.

50

Mike, my son Jon, and I are standing on the shoulder of a road on the north side of Duluth. There are others standing around too. Cars pass by, encouraged by the men swinging flashlights in the dark. Other men fling shovelfuls of snow onto the road and smack them down, trying to keep a snowy track for the anticipated dogsled. We ask some race officials standing behind us when they think the first sled will come through, and they say, "Anytime." So we stand and stare into the dark forest, waiting for some sign that they're coming. I jump up and down to keep warm.

Then someone says, "She's coming!" and we can see a small light appear and disappear among the trees. Now all the bystanders move onto the road and form two lines, one on either side of the snow track. This is done so that the dogs don't try to go running down the road. First the dogs come into view and people start cheering and clapping, and then we see the sled with the musher on the back and the cheers get louder. The dogs' eyes light up in the flash of a camera. They keep moving, although one right in front of the sled seems to think this is the stopping point and starts to lag. I hear Jamie say, "I'm going to push you all the way, if I have to," and she nudges it with the front of the sled. The dog comes to its senses and they're off into the darkness again.

The two lines disintegrate and people go back to the side of the road. The next musher is supposed to be only three minutes behind, so we stand and watch for the beam to appear. Three minutes pass, five, eight, and finally ten. I see a momentary spark of light high up among the trees and say, "He's coming." Mike and Jon look and so do others, but they don't see the light. I'm sure I saw it, and before I start to feel really foolish, someone further up the hill sees him coming. Again the two lines form on the road. Again, we clap and cheer as the dogs and Robin cross the road. Someone tells him as he passes that he's eleven minutes behind the leader. That's got to be discouraging at this point in the race.

As he rushes away, we run back to the car and head for the finish line at Lester Park. The streets are lined with cars and there are people streaming up the road. It's 1:15 A.M. We park the car and run to the area where the crowd waits. An announcer says, "They should be arriving momentarily." It's a carnival mob scene. People bundled in snowmobile suits, down parkas, fur caps, Sorrel boots, all mill around. Big spotlights light up the finish line and the area behind it. Officials walk around carrying clipboards. The fans line the orange snow fence and stand on the bleachers placed along the sides.

We walk up past the finish gate and stand on the packed snowbanks to watch and wait. The digital clock says 1:34 A.M. when the first wave of sound lifts ahead of us. We pick up the clapping and cheering as Jamie Nelson and her seven hardy dogs come down the chute. There is a smile on Jamie's face that competes with the brightness of the spotlights. She is enveloped by media and handlers and race people. It's hard to see the dogs, for all the people. We feel happiness for her and relief after such a long, hard race. We also feel sorry for the team coming in ten minutes later. He also has run a hard race, but there will be little satisfaction with second place.

We clap and cheer as he goes by, but there is no beaming grin on his face. He smiles, but it is resignation and probably relief to have finished. He had a dog quit on him after one checkpoint and had to carry it back and start over, costing him precious minutes, possibly race-winning time.

The next racer isn't expected for two hours or more, and so we mingle with the crowd around Jamie's truck and dogs. Her 14-year-old son Eric is there—he came in third in the 130-mile race.

Then it's back to the car and a drive home in the wee hours. But we saw the finish of a challenge to human and animal spirit. We saw people who had become real to us, after seeing and meeting them at Sawbill on Thursday. We saw the looks of satisfaction and pride that are well deserved after five hundred-mile, five-day race in the middle of January, along a rugged, winding, spectacular coastline.

Bohemian waxwings are found along the North Shore in winter. One of their favorite foods is the fruit of the mountain ash. (D. Cox)

SKI TRAILS

BY KATE CROWLEY

It was a sparkling winter day when four of us piled into Bill's truck for a ride up to County Road 45, where the cross-country ski trail intersects the road.

Since purchasing Solbaakens Resort, Bill and Beth Blank have immersed themselves in the community, ecology, and culture of the North Shore, and they have been leaders in the development of the North Shore Mountain Ski Trail. Through a cooperative effort with the U.S. Forest Service, Minnesota DNR, North Star Ski Club, and private resort owners, the trail system has grown to more than two hundred kilometers.

As we turned to ascend the hill to our takeoff point, Bill talked about the conditions we could expect. "It should be pretty good right now. The temperatures have been cold, and with the recent snowfall, the tracks should be well set."

This would be my first experience cross-country skiing in these inland "mountains." The highlands are not mountains when compared to the western peaks, but they are not glacial hills either. This is bedrock country, with structural elevation changes that make the Sawtooth Range the tallest in Minnesota. Their highest points cause us to gasp, not because of lack of oxygen, but because of the beauty spread before us. My companions were more familiar with these trails, and they were anxious to get underway. While I was infected by their excitement, I also had a few butterflies fluttering around inside, in anticipation of the unknown.

Bill dropped us off with a wish for a good time, and then we were alone at the trailhead, with more than four miles to travel downhill to the truck that was parked near Cascade State Park.

A two-way track was well set, and David and Froydis, the younger and more experienced skiers, were gone with a whoop and a holler. I let Mike go before me so that I could slow down when necessary and not block someone coming up from behind. I really had no idea about what sort of grade to expect. The entire trail system has been designed for the beginner/intermediate, with more difficult loops well marked. This trail had both "most difficult" and "more difficult" signs printed on the map.

After a few easy turns through the trees, the trail opened up to a magnificent vista of the great blue lake. Standing there momentarily to drink in the view, I wondered where else a person could stand on skis and stare off into an unending stretch of water, as big as an inland sea.

This type of setting and skiing was especially rewarding for Froydis, for it reminded her of her homeland—Norway. She grew up on skis; looking at her blond hair and handknit sweater and mittens, I could easily picture her schussing down a mountainside, with a fjord below.

After a few minutes, I began to feel more comfortable with the trail and my ability to handle it. Relaxing generally improves one's skiing. Loosening up allows the skier to absorb the dips and take the turns more fluidly.

After a section of trail that included some nice curves and drops, we came to a long, straight stretch that provided me with the most outright fun ride I've ever taken on a pair of skis. The slope was gradual, but gravity and momentum worked together.

Gaining speed, I crouched lower and tucked my poles deeper under my arms. We were into the trees and still going downhill. I was laughing for joy and the feeling of wild recklessness, tears streaming down my cheeks. The track was icy in places and my skis rattled and bounced. I prayed that they wouldn't leave the track.

A sign flashed by, warning of a cross-trail up ahead, but I didn't have time or space to slow down, so I just hoped no one was coming through. I yelled out a warning as I approached and shot through the intersection. Still no end in sight, although the grade was leveling out, so I tucked a little tighter and pumped up and down as I passed over some slight bumps.

Then I saw the clearing and the sign indicating the trail's end. What exhilaration, what a sense of accomplishment!

David and Froydis were already there waiting, and

The North Shore Mountain Ski Trail offers miles of beginner and intermediate groomed cross-country ski trails and unlimited beauty. (M. Link)

Mike came down last. He was as excited by the run as I was and suggested we walk back up and do it again. I didn't have enough energy to go all the way back, but it was worth a try. We went back, breathing hard at the top, and flew down once again, only this time I ended up on my side in a snowbank. Even that was fun on this day.

* * *

Four years later, Mike and I returned to Solbaakens with two other friends. Snow conditions weren't as ideal as the first time and Gisela had not been cross-country skiing for several years. She stayed in a snow-plow much of the way, but on several occasions, her ski tips crossed and she somersaulted and rolled downhill. Laughing, even after breaking a pair of sun-glasses, she got back up and gamely continued down.

Mike was having a rough day too. One of his bind-ings was not working properly, which he discovered when he left the trail and plowed into deeper snow. Instead of stopping, he was propelled headlong on one ski into a clump of bushes. Not seeing the accident take place, I came up from behind and saw him stand-ing and replacing his skis, so I slowed down a bit, said "Howdy," and continued on. Little did I know he was in a daze and seeing stars.

The day was beautiful, with temperatures in the high thirties and a bright, shining blue sky. We stopped to look out at the metallic shimmer on the lake, and Gisela and Muzzy marveled at the view, as I had done on my first trip. Muzzy is an avid pho-tographer, and the day provided him with lots of op-portunities. On the flatter stretches we looked at lightly indented tracks left by wolves and deep holes punched into the snow by moose. There were grouse tracks snaking out from the bushes, and in a few places we could see the imprint of wingtips where a bird had lifted into flight.

Overhead, the chattering sound of gray jays erupt-ed and floated into the great open sky. Winter birds do not sing like spring migrants; they are too intent on survival to celebrate with song. However, the winter air tends to be stiller, crisp, more conducive to the movement of sound. No broad leaves absorb or block the vibrations of bird sound, so we hear more than we could in other seasons.

When we pause, the nasal honk of the nuthatches, the sassy notes of the chickadees, and the buzz of siskins and waxwings seem to enliven the forest. Nuthatches scour the trunks of the trees, part of the "bark-gleaning guild" that includes woodpeckers and brown creepers. Purple finches, redpolls, and tree sparrows are out on the branches shaking the seeds loose from birch catkins, while crossbills open the sticky scales of pinecones with their offset beaks and remove the seeds.

Flocks of Bohemian waxwings move to mountain maple and other fruits that stay through the winter, and grosbeaks use their strong mandibles to crunch seeds. The evening grosbeaks travel in boisterous flocks, while the sedate pine grosbeaks are in smaller groups on the edge of trails and roads. Each bird is a combination of color, sound, and energy that gives the winter landscape added beauty.

The pleasures of cross-country skiing include deciphering the stories left in the snow by the winter residents of the woods and stopping to listen to and observe the birds. Animals often take advantage of the ski trails too, since they provide good perches and an energy-saving path to travel.

Two does groom one another, a common social interaction among white-tail deer. (D. Cox)

NORTH SHORE DEER

BY MIKE LINK

The North Shore is not only a land of rugged rock coasts, massive wave energy, plunging rivers, and scenic lighthouses. It is also an area of unusual ecology. The high rocky shoulders of the lake face south at an angle that catches the warmth of the winter sun. Lake Superior seldom freezes, so it is a radiant source of thirty-two degrees above zero, while the land behind the ridges may plunge to thirty-two below (or more).

From ridge top to lakeshore is a zone with moderate winter weather and just enough snow to insulate and protect new plant growth, without impeding wildlife movement. This is an ecological tension zone from one-half to two miles wide and two hundred miles long, where white-tailed deer congregate in the winter.

Prior to 1910, this area was home to moose, caribou, wolf, and a few deer. Then large-scale logging came to the North Shore forest. In its wake, second-growth forests of birch, aspen, maple, fir, and spruce took over. Moose and caribou, whose needs are not met by such a forest, declined, but white-tailed deer increased dramatically, to as many as five hundred per square mile in the "deer yards" between Lutsen and Grand Marais. (In the winter, deer gather in deer yards, places where they can find food, follow in one another's tracks in the snow, and in groups find some safety from predators. Wolves can concentrate on a single deer; but a large group of deer can divide the wolves' attention, giving the deer a head start in the snow.)

The moose and the caribou could not survive in this situation for many reasons. The most lethal reason was a parasite called brain worm, which survives in white-tailed deer without harming them. The parasite passes through the deer and enters the waters of the region, where snails ingest one form of the life cycle. The snails are then eaten by moose when they eat aquatic vegetation. In the moose, the parasite matures and attacks the motor region of the brain. The infected animal will wander aimlessly until its dies. Some infected moose have been found grazing with cows in a pasture, or wandering in southern Minnesota and Iowa. With too many white-tails, the moose cannot survive.

The caribou were harmed by logging because of the destruction of old-growth forest and the lichen crops that grow there. Their food was eliminated by the change in forest; at the same time, they became food for the loggers. The caribou were gone from the northern forests by the mid 1920s.

The number of deer expanded until they overgrazed their range, and the second-growth post-logging forest gradually matured. In the 1960s, the deer population began to drop, until the winter populations numbered 100 to 125 deer per square mile.

The deer adapted to the changing conditions in several ways. Their favorite foods in the area were white cedar and mountain ash, but overgrazing eliminated those from the regular diet. Mountain ash need precarious rock footholds to get established. When they reach the height where they stick out of the snow cover, they are quickly eaten.

White cedar is also called arborvitae, the "tree of life," because it has so much ability to reproduce. If a tree falls, each branch grows upward to form a line of new trees. If a lower branch is partially covered with leaves and debris, it forms new roots and begins another tree. The tree has been prized for many commercial purposes, but it grows very slowly and that has made it unpopular for reforestation.

Its slow growth also means that seedlings cannot escape the ravages of the white-tailed browsers. White cedar has been a major part of the forest, and there are still large stands along the highway, but the stands are all old growth, not new seedlings. To the deer, white cedar is gourmet dining, and they avail themselves of every available morsel. That's why the North Shore trees are all old, and why they appear to wear miniskirts that expose their trunks—that is the height the deer can reach.

In one obscure open area in Cascade State Park, I found a patch of very small white cedars. It was a grove of twelve-inch trees with clusters of branches

A hard winter with lots of snowfall may mean that some fawns will not survive. This is nature's way of balancing population with the available food supply. (D. Cox)

so dense that the scale-like leaves grew in vertical columns, like playing cards arranged in a circle around the trunk—a bonzai arrangement created by the constant pruning of the upward growth. Then a series of light snow years exposed the grove, and the entire patch disappeared.

In the present forest, the deer survive on the abundance of a shrub, the mountain maple, which seems to flourish with pruning, sending up two branches where one was snipped back. Up to a point, it can maintain itself with constant annual pruning of seventy to ninety percent. This is the understory plant that gives the autumn woods the red glow.

Another deer adaptation for the northern climes is a pattern of migration. They move as far as thirty-five miles from winter to summer feeding territories. Summer dispersal is important because no ecological area can sustain concentrations like those in the deer yards. The dispersal spreads the deer out. This also helps them avoid a concentration that would encourage predators during their fawning period. It makes them less susceptible to disease, and gives them a varied diet.

They move to the North Shore again as the snow falls. Since conifers are low on the preferred food list, the spruce, fir, and pine of the interior make poor grazing for winter survival. In addition, the snows get too deep away from the lake, and the deer will flounder. On the shore, the deciduous growth aids the slopes in getting maximum solar energy, which keeps the snow cover from getting too deep but offers very little protection during a snow storm.

The deer turn to the valley conifers for their shelter during winter storms. Under the conifers the snow cover is diminished. The needle-covered branches intercept the falling snow and shelter the sleeping deer until the sun can settle the fresh cover in the surrounding woods. Studies of the area show that the cedar not

A white-tail fawn lies motionless and relies on a camouflaged coat to protect it from predators. (D. Cox)

only is the best food but in its mature form makes the best roof too.

Along with the rise in deer populations, the wolf has prospered. The wolf population is limited by its food source. The moose and caribou are difficult to catch; the deer population expanded quickly and is much easier prey, so the North Shore wolf packs grew, with the pack around Cascade State Park numbering more than a dozen.

These wolves have howled for me during midday skiing of the trails, adding to the charm of the area. Their tracks indicate that they tend to break the large pack up into smaller hunting parties to work the yard. These wolves are not harming the deer population; in fact the deer are still too numerous in this area. Deer numbers are limited by food, not predation.

Off the highway, there are some old deer exclosures that have kept them from munching the new growth. I visited one that was still fenced, and it was impres-

sive to see the lush area, surrounded by a very open woodlot.

North of Grand Marais, moose roam, and deer are not as common. Bears are scattered all along the shore, and furbearers like marten, mink, weasel, and otter are located along the rivers and throughout the forests. There are squirrels, chipmunks, porcupines, and skunks. The ecology of the North Shore has a full array of mammals.

In the early 1980s, two woodland caribou wandered down the North Shore highway all the way to Grand Marais. Were they Canadian sightseers or real estate speculators? Maybe they were a signal to us that the shore can return gracefully to the wilderness it once was, with some deer, some moose, a few packs of wolves, and even a few woodland caribou.

The Brule River charges through narrow basalt walls and drops into the Devil's Kettle. (B. Firth)

JUDGE C.R. MAGNEY STATE PARK

BY KATE CROWLEY

It takes some commitment to visit Judge C. R. Magney Park. It is the last state park along the North Shore, eighteen miles north of Grand Marais, but it is the park I have visited most often.

The Brule River churns and twists through the steep rock walls, and the hiking trails parallel the water. Most of my visits to Magney have occurred in the fall or winter, and so when I think of the park, I associate it with heavy gray skies. But the cloud cover has always seemed appropriate, for it focuses the attention on the land and the water, rather than on the brilliant blue of a clear sky.

My first trip to Magney was in late October, when two naturalist friends and I decided to take a short break from work and families. The bright colors of autumn were long past and the gray of late fall was prominent. The morning after our arrival, we awoke to cloudy skies and temperatures in the forties. We bundled up for a day's worth of hiking and set off.

The trail to the Devil's Kettle was narrow and muddy in places, with tree roots and rounded rocks sticking out waiting to trip us. We were forced to pay more attention to our footing than to the surrounding forest, but we could smell, and listen, and the cloud cover facilitated both senses. The humidity was high, and the smell of the spruce trees permeated the air and made us aware of our proximity to the great boreal forests. The loud sound of the river rushing below was constant.

A few birds were in evidence. The black-capped chickadees flew from branch to branch and called out warnings of our approach. A pileated woodpecker must have heard the alarm, for we saw a flash of black, white, and red flying through the trees, trailed by a flickerlike hysterical call.

Not long after the woodpecker passed, a ruffed grouse burst out of the brush, and before we had a chance to gasp, it was gone. I really think these birds should be called "cardiac-arrest birds," for their unexpected and explosive takeoffs. It may be a quick means of escape from a predator, but flying in thick timber also has inherent risks. They have been known to hit branches and lose their lives through the impact.

Along the North Shore, ruffed grouse are limited by the forest makeup. They depend heavily on aspen trees for food and shelter. The best aspen stands are produced in forests where there is frequent, cyclic change, brought on by forest fire, wind damage, or logging. At this time the amount of aspen regeneration is low; as a result, the ruffed grouse population is low too. Good grouse habitat is hard to find along the North Shore.

Further up the trail, we found evidence of an old forest fire. The blackened, jagged stump of a great old pine grabbed our attention. It had a beautiful abstract design created by combination of the charred bark and the exposed and aging inner trunk, which was striped in shades of brown and grey. The remaining bark resembled charcoal.

As the trail turned and sloped downward, we encountered a fine mist, and then foaming white water, tumbling over a black lava drop. Near the edge the spray coated our faces and clothes, and transfixed us with its power and fury.

Above the falls is a cliff edge, where we could observe the water disappearing into a hole in the basalt streambed. This is the Devil's Kettle. From this vantage point we could look up the river, along its rock-strewn bed and beyond, to the mix of bare birch trees and pointed dark-green spruce.

The combination of sights and sounds epitomized the north country to me. It captured the spirit of Judge Clarence R. Magney, a Minnesota State Supreme Court justice, who earlier in this century recognized the irreplaceable beauty and value of the North Shore. Because of his vision and commitment to preserving public lands, many wayside rests and parks were established. In honor of his work and dedication, this 4,500-acre park was named for him.

At the end of our October trip, my two friends and I made a pact to return together to this special place.

Six years later, we made our return pilgrimage and brought along two more friends. We arrived late at night, but spent some time warming up around the

Black-capped chickadees observed Kate and her friends and warned other woodland creatures of their approach. (D. Cox)

Pine grosbeak (L. Rogers)

A white-throated sparrow is not as colorful as a warbler, but its melodious call of "O' my Canada, Canada, Canada" is a soothing refrain at dawn and dusk. (D. Cox)

massive stone fireplace of Naniboujou Lodge and planning our next day. In the morning, under a snow-colored sky, we prepared for our hike to the Devil's Kettle. Without snowshoes, the walking was slow.

We had dressed warmly, anticipating the cold morning, but after ten minutes of struggling through the calf-deep snow, we were unzipping jackets and loosening scarves. The uphill trail, which normally provides good exercise, was especially challenging. We made frequent stops to catch our breath and let our pulses return to normal. The sound of blood pounding in our ears nearly drowned out the overwhelming silence.

We saw a few hairy and downy woodpeckers working their way up the trunks of some birch trees. Lying on top of the undisturbed snow were the tiny seeds of both the paper and yellow birch. The yellow birch seed is shaped like a perfect fleur-de-lis, while the white birch seed is shaped more like a bird in flight. The seeds, packed closely together on the dangling catkins, are freed by foraging finches and dis-

persed by the winter winds.

A pair of loud croaking ravens flew overhead and broke the silence. Below us a gentle chorus of water bubbled under and over breaks in the ice.

A great dome of ice and snow had built up over the rapids at the base of the falls. The water still flowed, the color of weak tea with milk, over the drop, and then disappeared under the dome. We gingerly tested the strength of the snow bubble and, feeling adventurous, crawled up its side and sat like mountaineers at the summit for a group photo.

Three of us climbed the last stretch of trail to look down at the black pool of water in the Devil's Kettle. A massive drapery of ice and snow spilled down to the water, and we could see movement under the more transparent ice. Looking beyond, as we had done six years earlier, we saw the river as a curving bed of white, broken by a snakelike track of water. The hills were a mix of grey, deep-green and white, and a quiet wilderness world surrounded these happy explorers.

GRAND PORTAGE

BY MIKE LINK

Paddling in a Montreal canoe is unlike any other boat experience. Nothing fancy, just stroke, stroke, stroke, to the French chansons.

Men and beaver pelts, blankets and rum, flour, beans, and pork are loaded into a large birchbark canoe with no room to stand or move around. The front paddler sets the pace, the rear paddler sings and steers, and the rest paddle. They don't switch sides and they don't change beats. From dawn until dusk all they get is a pipe break once an hour and a bowl of beans for breakfast. It brings to mind the oarsmen on the galley ships, except the voyageurs chose their life willingly.

The voyageur is the colorful character of the mid-continent, the predecessor to the gunfighter and frontiersman. French Canadian paddlers with their own accents and slang, enough to confuse people in both Montreal and Paris, were the dominant non-Indians in the land of lakes. They were the change makers, the importers of western culture to Indian outposts.

They adapted quickly to Indian language, Indian wives, the canoe and snowshoe, and the general lifestyle of the Native American. They wore colorful sashes wrapped around their waists and their legs, toted ninety pound packs, and seldom saw their own homes.

The caste system included the pork eaters, who paddled the big lake; the winterers, who lived inland; and the Athabascans, who were the supermen of the trade.

Legends of black voyageurs, prodigious volumes of beaver carried over portages, sunken boats on inland rapids, cargoes that disappeared in lake storms, and an annual blood sacrifice to the hordes of mosquitoes, blackflies, no-see-ums, deerflies, stable flies, and horseflies all add color and awe to the tales. Voyageurs rubbed skunk oil and bear grease on their bodies to keep away the insects, and they survived on foods with names like pemmican and rubbaboo.

Coming to Grand Portage for the annual rendezvous, the men of the Northwest Company were per-forming a ritual of the lake country that started with Jean Nicolet, who carried a Chinese robe to wear when he crossed the big lakes just in case he reached China on the other side. There were men like Radisson and Groseilliers, occasionally called Radishes and Gooseberries. Groseilliers was the educated explorer, while his partner had once been kidnapped by Mohawks, with whom he lived and even joined raiding parties before escaping. His life was one of torture, adventure, and hardship.

The first paddlers after the Indians were courier du bois, men of the woods, often going into the country illegally (they required licenses even in those days). In their wake was a succession of forts, with La Pointe on Madeline Island in the Apostle Islands, followed by Fond du Lac in Duluth, and then Grand Portage.

The Great Lakes extended a promising water route into the very middle of the continent. It seemed to be a siren call to those who could not get rid of northwest passage fever. More important, it led the entrepreneur to the lakes and beavers, and the trader then introduced commerce.

Beavers were the motivation for trade; other pelts were secondary. Vanity was the stimulus that gave the beaver its allure—felt hats of beaver pelt, potions of beaver castoreum to stimulate the brain, dreams of fortune with two buck teeth. A succession of areas was opened, and each time the beaver was trapped out, so that new places were needed. It was not manifest destiny in the north, it was a trapper's trail.

Today there is a national monument, stark walls of sharpened tree trunks and a longhouse that is a mute symbol of raucous days when the fort walls were needed to keep the drunken traders out, rather than to protect them within. It was a time for bragging, fighting, and drinking. It was not high society. The only skills that counted among the paddlers were endurance, strength, and the ability to believe that you were stronger, faster, and a better paddler than anyone else. The term *macho* was not in use on this border, but

Furs of all kinds were sought and traded by the voyageurs, but none were as highly valued as the skins of the beaver, which was transformed into a fashionable top hat. (S. Kuchera)

65

The American Fur Company built this fort at Grand Portage in the 1700s and then forced the Northwest Company to move its operations into Canada and to build Fort William. (S. Kuchera)

The Witch Tree stands alone, a mystical, spiritual reminder of the bond between the earth and the Ojibwa Indians. (S. Kuchera)

the term *voyageur* meant the same thing.

Behind the post is the actual portage, a nine-mile trail that leads from Lake Superior to the Pigeon River. Today it leads to the Canadian border, but back then it was a passage to inland riches and the real test of manhood, the challenge of overwintering in the interior.

Walking the trail today is a wonderful experience, and many people use backpacks so that they can camp on the riverside before returning to the post. In the 1700s, they carried watersoaked canoes and ninety-pound packs across the trail, up and down hills, over fallen logs, and through muddy lowspots.

They fastened their packs by a tumpline that went over the forehead, and if they were real men, they would take more than one pack at a time. They did not walk, they trotted, probably to get it over with, so they could stop the suffering and scratch all the accumulated insect bites. They did not camp when they got to the end, either; they hurried back to carry another load. That is what makes the portage so "grand."

Moccasined feet gave way to Vibram soles, and then to low-impact hiking boots. The trail was established by forgotten Indians, who did not know that they were leading a historic parade. Today's hiker takes this trail for the feeling of history more than for the abundance of nature that is all along the path.

The French Canadians held the post until 1805, when it passed into the possession of the United States and the Canadian Northwest Company went north hoping to find an acceptable pathway to the interior. In 1808, the American Fur Company came in and tried to survive as a fishing post. From 1805 on, the post had little significance.

The fur trade was a Canadian industry. In the fur trade lineage, trading had been dominated by the XY Company, the Northwest Company, and the Hudson Bay Company. The American Fur Company made its fortunes in the mountains, not the lakes. When Astor began to operate in this arena, he and his partners referred to the regional operation as the South West Company. It may be the only time in history that Minnesota has been in the southwest.

THE WITCH TREE

In Ojibwa legend, the spirit Nanaboujou was forced from the earth to reside on an island in the east. The sunset represents death, and Nanaboujou was still alive, so he was sent to the sunrise. We now know the "island" as the Sibley Peninsula in Ontario.

In Francis Densmore's classic studies of the Ojibwa, she tells the legend of Winabojo (another name for Nanaboujou) and the cedar tree. We learn that he is wearing a cedar tree on his head, as an ornament, with the roots all around him. The cedar has been known as a tree of life in many cultures, a fact that stems from its ability to withstand so many setbacks and still keep growing.

On the east side (the sunrise side) of Hat Point, a sacred, gnarled, twisted white cedar grows. Bonsai-like sculpturing has left this twisted wood with its green topknot perched ten feet above the water and isolated from the surrounding forest. Its roots twine around the rocks, and sacred bundles of tobacco are tucked into its limbs and back. This is the witch tree, perhaps the most famous tree on Lake Superior. It is between 250 and 400 years old, and it appears as though there is no soil to nourish any of its roots. La Vérendrye is supposed to have seen this tree in 1731. It is in the shadow of Mount Josephine and overlooks the waters of Waswaugonig Bay.

Both the Cree and the Ojibwa have used this spirit (manitou) tree for offerings. In a mix of legends, the tree was the abode of an evil spirit in the form of a large bird of prey that would swamp canoes. I wonder if the bird might not have been an osprey, which perched on the branches and plunged from the air while fishing. It might have seemed like it was trying to bomb the canoe.

The tree's importance to us is the feeling of walking through a moss-covered forest to the wave-washed rock coast and there encountering a tree with a startling and spiritual impact. It is part of the religion of the Indians who inhabited the land and it is still a manitou. The spirit of this tree is the rugged spirit of both the people and the coast. It is Nanaboujou's ornament.

Isle Royale is a national park with wind and wave-swept shorelines. They are a test for a sailor's courage and navigational skills. (B. Firth)

ISLE ROYALE UNDER SAIL

BY MIKE LINK

We took our sitings on the lights from Devil's Island and Outer Island and established a "line of travel" for the night. This was the beginning of a crossing; soon the lights would disappear behind the curve of the earth, and we would be alone on the big lake, with our wits responsible for delivering us and the forty-two-foot ketch *Izmir* to Isle Royale. The sun set as we cruised between Outer Island and Cat Island in the Apostle Islands National Lakeshore. We were traveling from national park to national park.

Our ship's log now included speed, distance, time, and direction. We would be checking them regularly and watching for lights as we approached the Minnesota shore. We would watch the stars, and the sky would dominate our experience.

The moon seemed to rise right out of the water, and we would not have been surprised to see a line of rain beneath it, like the droplets that fall off a beach ball when it is taken from the water. But there would be no droplets—it was mere illusion, a 220,000-mile juxtaposition. The moon continued to rise as orange and round as a Halloween pumpkin, then gradually changed to a whiteness that set the waters glowing and sparkling.

Moonglow shut out the light from eastern stars, but not Jupiter. The planet was low on the horizon and beckoned like a celestial lighthouse. The spectacular display made the trip somewhat like sailing in a planetarium. Northern lights radiated in three separate arcs, mirrored in the waters, and we experienced a beautiful meteor shower, with one brilliant flare that turned green as it burned out near the horizon.

The crew went to bed between 11 P.M. and midnight, and the sky lost its intensity about the same time. Sky and sea became one, a ball of darkness, a swirling mass in all directions. The wind picked up, and we moved under full sails until the wind swung directly into our face from the northeast. The chop grew to waves, and the people sleeping in the "V" berth were flipped like pancakes.

The two hours just before sunrise were the most difficult. It wasn't the waves, but the tedium of light-less concentration. There were slight wind shifts to adjust to, the constant correction for wave orientation, and the internal battle to stay awake. Then the sun rose. A wash of orange spread across the entire eastern horizon, and Venus and Mercury accompanied the sun the way Jupiter had followed the moon. Celestial remoras.

By now the waves were three to five feet, and the horizon would rise and lower with each crest. From the bow, the waves disappeared below and then quickly washed the deck as the boat rose and plunged. It was there that I first glimpsed the island on the horizon. Contact. Isle Royale.

Our dead reckoning was right on. Plunging and surging, waves separated by our bow sprayed both port and starboard. We felt a mood of festivity, and enough elation to want to go below deck and cook in the jostling galley.

The big lake is intimidating. It moves most birds around the shorelines instead of across it (although a yellowthroat intercepted us, and after flying around the boat twice, it landed on deck for a breather). For years the lake had pushed me around the shorelines too, but now I felt tremendous satisfaction in the crossing. With a strong headwind blocking our progress, we took tacks with the deck at waterline until we reached Washington Harbor.

Approaching Isle Royale from this direction, you first see a single land mass; then as you get nearer, it becomes an entire grouping of islands, an archipelago. Isle Royale is one large island, but there are approximately two hundred little islands around and within the big one. Near Rock of Ages lighthouse, the water is littered with rocks just at or near the surface, rocks that threaten every boat that attempts to navigate the island. The lighthouse is much more than a spectacle—it is a necessity.

The island is a haven from storm if you can get to it, but Isle Royale is also a garden of shipwrecks. Perhaps the most accessible shipwreck in the lake is the *America*, which rests under two to eighty-five feet of water, with its upper portions visible in the clear lake

Sunset on Isle Royale. (J. and A. Mahan)

waters. Among the rocks are three more wrecks, two wooden steamers and a steel passenger vessel. They are all good dives, but to a sailor who is just seeking port, they are also ghostly marks on the navigational chart.

There is nothing soft about this park. It is a land of harshness, wind- and wave-swept shorelines, northern coldness and snows, and ancient rocks that have resisted the advances of milleniums of natural forces. The rocks here are Precambrian, which means beyond the age of our comprehension. They are the same ages as the shoreline volcanics, part of the same events and energies that have created the falls and headlands of the North Shore and the Keewanaw Peninsula.

They are lavas with names, like Minong Flow and Tobin Harbor Flow, that reflect the geologist's reference points. Within the rocks are green semiprecious stones, chlorastrolites (green stars), more commonly called greenstones. This small gemstone fades in the sunlight; perhaps it is the one weak part of the island. But there is also the Greenstone Ridge, the backbone of the island, which forms the interior highlands and Mounts Desor, Sugar, and Siskiwit. Unlike the gems, this is tough rock that has absorbed the impact of thousands of Vibram soles, in addition to the onslaught of weather.

Like waves in the lake, the various flows (there are eleven on the geologic map) line up in parallel lines. The geological map is an artistic creation, a color rendition of millions of years of crustal formation and deformity. There are color contrasts and color coordinates. Green, blue, and yellow lavas are predominant, and the orange of the Feldtman Ridge stands out. This is the younger rock, the conglomerate rock, made of weathered fragments of the older formations.

It is an island of faults, those deep incisions into the

70

The graves of early settlers are one of the clues to human history on the island. (B. Firth)

rock that have allowed movement. One side of the break may have moved, both sides may have changed places, or the missing area between two valley walls may be the part that moved. Faults are not like human faults, problems to be corrected; they are statements about the land, and locations where the bedrock relieves the various stresses it is subject to.

The Minong Ridge is incised with numerous parallel faults, all of which cross the ridge and make the hiker go down and then back up in going from Washington Harbor to Tobin Harbor. On the Greenstone Ridge, the major faults contain Chickenbone and Hatchet Lakes. The bottoms of the faults are beaver and moose meadows, wet and spongy. The sides of the faults are steep and the occasional use of hands on the trail is called for. On top, the rock is exposed and is often hot and dry.

The ridges and the valleys, the moisture and the dryness, all contribute to the complex nature of this International Biosphere Preserve. It is a natural laboratory, a window into the ecology of Lake Superior. Naturalists, scientists, environmentalists, sailors, divers—we all study this island. We extract from it images and understanding, we take home beauty and knowledge. We are challenged not only to get here, but to look once we arrive.

But we are not the first to arrive. There were birchbark crafts that ventured here long before sailboats. The Indians were drawn by copper deposits, which lie in pockets between the layers of rock. They extracted ore, but they did not stay. Others followed for ore and for timber, for fish and for solitude. The progression of humans does not diminish this park's wilderness; they add to its ecological story.

ISLE ROYALE ON THE WING

BY KATE CROWLEY

Whenever a person recalls a wilderness backpack trip, he or she views a mental kaleidoscope of grand scenery, weather good and bad, and some of the more physically challenging moments. We forget the moment-to-moment visions that are presented as we place one foot in front of the other and try to find a more comfortable position for a pack that seems to grow heavier with each step. It is only in rereading my journals that I am reminded of the small, beautiful, fleeting sounds and sights that surround the hiker.

A great percentage of the hiking trails on Isle Royale are enclosed by dense stands of trees. The sweeping panoramic views come from the exposed, rocky ridges. But then it's back down again into the dark-green concealing forest.

Like most people who come to Isle Royale, I have always hoped to see or hear a wolf, and I have been thrilled by any encounter with a moose. But when I replay memories from my visits to the island, the images that shine in living color, that bring me right back to the moment on the trail or campsite, are the ones that feature the winged inhabitants of the forest and field.

* * *

It was mid-July and the peak of the flowering season. The season of butterflies. I was walking on the trail to the office at Windigo and the breeze was carrying the perfume of the ninebark shrubs. The anthers of the ninebark flower sit atop long filaments, where any insect that lands will brush against them and aid in pollination. The white umbel-shaped flowers were spilling over green leaves and attracting more than my attention. A tiger swallowtail, with pale yellow wings etched and outlined with black lines, had just settled lightly on a cluster of white petals. It may have been probing for nectar, or it may have just been soaking up the midday sun.

On the trail to Hugginin Cove, I was stopped in my tracks by the sight of three bright orange fritillary butterflies, each daintily perched on a hawkweed flower. Were they drawn to those flowers because they so perfectly match one another in color? Swaying in synchronization with the light breeze, a painted lady clung to the purple topknot of the knapweed flower.

Butterflies inspire feelings of lightness and hope in us. They make a summer day dreamlike. They have many of the same features that people find ugly and frightening on other insects, but all we ever really see are their tissue-thin intricately patterned wings. We marvel at how these delicate winged beauties seem to appear out of the summer sky, perform their pollinating flights, and then disappear for another year.

Because we know so little about their lives and travels, it is easy to forget that they live in a threatened world. The butterfly is part of the ecology of this biosphere preserve. A survey taken on the island during the summer of 1986 catalogued thirty-two different species of moths and butterflies. They have special habitat needs, and with every new housing or industrial development they lose a little more ground. The Nature Conservancy has preserved special tracts of land specifically for some of these mysterious and ephemeral bits of life.

One afternoon at my shelter in the Washington Creek campground, I laid two pairs of sweaty hiking socks on the picnic table to dry and I sat down nearby to read a book in the warm sun. A white admiral (banded purple) butterfly swooped in and landed on the socks. This butterfly is black, with prominent white bands and subtle red spots and iridescent blue on the hind wings.

Shortly after the first butterfly landed, it was joined by another. They sat on the socks with their three inches of wings pumping up and down. Then another landed, and another. Before long, there were six white admirals finding some unknown pleasure on my socks. If I approached too closely for a look, they fluttered up, swirled about, and landed back on the socks when I sat back down.

It's still a mystery to me. Were they attracted to the bright white color in that midday light? Was it some

Osprey are large birds of prey that are found near lakes and streams of Isle Royale. Their stick nests are built high in nearby trees, and fish make up the majority of their diet. (J. and A. Mahan)

73

fragrance my socks were broadcasting? Was it salt they were seeking, or just moisture? Whatever it was, it completely occupied them and me for almost an hour.

While I watched the socks, three of the butterflies drifted over and landed on me. I watched them move on thread-like legs across the skin on my arm, legs, and toes, too light to be felt. As they walked, they probed with their long tongues curling and uncurling. They're probably the only insect we don't automatically brush away. In fact, we do just the opposite — we pray they'll stay so we can watch them longer. I wondered what would be a good descriptive word for a group of butterflies. A flutter? A fugue?

Gradually, they lost interest and flew away one by one, apparently satiated, my socks dry and me full of wonder.

* * *

A friend and I started the day in McCargo Cove, hiked along the Minong Ridge to Todd Harbor, and then decided to take the branching trail into Hatchet Lake. It had been an easy day's hike, only seven miles, and we hadn't hurried. A young bull moose had stood on the trail from Todd Harbor and slowed our progress, but added excitement to the day's hike. By the time we got our camp set up, it was dinner time.

Hatchet Lake is small, and the camping area is set well within the trees of a sugar maple/yellow birch forest. It looked like a well-protected spot with a nice view of the lake.

Picture, if you will, an idyllic forest scene. Squirrels rustling in the leaves, birds singing, a glowing sunset dropping behind a pristine lake, and two campers contemplating the beauty of it all. In the background, you can hear the music slowly change from a soothing symphonic piece to the ominous beat of a horror movie.

In the forest, dusk came with amazing speed, and though the lake still reflected a pale light, our campsite was being enveloped by dark shadows. Without any warning, they attacked. The air vibrated with their bloodthirsty buzzing. Our safe, wind-protected campsite was the hideout for a nation of bloodthirsty terrorist mosquitoes.

We jumped about and flung our arms, trying to prevent any portion of our body from becoming a landing strip for the ravenous hordes. Our freeze-dried meal had not yet had time to complete its proper soaking and cooking period, but we couldn't possibly wait for it in this onslaught. We gathered utensils and survival gear, and with as little opening as possible, dove into the tent.

It was impossible to escape the murderous buggers without dragging a few in behind us in the vortex we created. We quickly fell upon those that had followed us in, squashing them on the tent walls and slapping them when they landed on us. Each death was a victory. It seemed as if we were making no dent in the population, and then we discovered the tiny holes in

the netting at the foot of the tent. A quick patching job sealed up the breaches in our defense. Finally, we looked around and felt sure that we were secure. Only then did we notice the tremendous humming sound above our heads.

The tent was the type with a screen top, which is great for star gazing and ventilation, but now it served as a thin barrier between us and our would-be tormentors. They hovered hungrily overhead, vainly poking their nasty little stingers into the mesh, hoping for a taste of us.

We couldn't completely tune them out, but we tried to ignore their noise as we turned to our meager and miserable meal. It was an awful concoction, purported to be vegie crepes. Even adding applesauce as a topping did nothing to improve the texture or taste. We were barely able to choke down a few spoonfuls of the pasty stuff. The combined effect of insect attack and food failure at the end of a day's hike was more stress than we could handle. Tempers began to flare, and since we were stuck for the evening in this confined spot, we each retreated into our own journal and reading material until it got too dark to see. The buzzing faded into the distance as sleep overtook us.

Before I fell asleep, I could see the bats swooping back and forth across the tent. I figured they must be just flying with their mouths open. We both woke at the same moment, to the same sound, and said, "What was that?" It was pitch black and even as our eyes adjusted to the darkness, another "thwump, swish" was heard.

Then we saw a bat barely visible in outline, land on our roof screen. The bats were landing either to rest or to eat the mosquitoes that were still trying to get us. They were the size of the little brown bat, and we were watching them in a rare display. "Plop, thump, swish" — they landed, took off, and sometimes missed and slid off the sides. We didn't dare cheer them on, for fear we'd scare them away, but we silently rejoiced at their hunt.

We watched until we fell asleep again. Morning arrived, and the buzzing of millions of mosquitoes was just as loud as the night before, but now it felt as though it was all inside my head. Had we really seen bats on our screen or were they just the dreams of the besieged? We emerged from our tent and felt grateful that we had chosen this spot, for what had started as an ambush of two unsuspecting hikers had overnight been transformed into a glimpse of the "enchanted forest."

* * *

It was mid July and the perfect afternoon for a easy hike to Hugginin Cove with just a light day pack on my back. I took time to stop and photograph a field full of daisies and hawkweed, to listen to woodpeckers tapping on trees, and to admire the scarlet fruit on the red-berried elder shrubs. As I walked deeper into the forest, red squirrels warned of my approach with their high pitched "*chrrrr*." Suddenly, over the squirrel

White admiral butterflies (D. Cox)

noise I heard another sound—loud, and similar to the ovenbird's, but different.

According to a 1966 Special Scientific report, there are 117 species of birds on Isle Royale during the summer. Thirty-three are considered common residents, 23 are rare, and the rest are described as uncommon.

On my visits to the Island, I have probably seen only 28 species, but when I am hiking with a heavy pack on my back, I don't usually have binoculars hanging around my neck or in easily accessible places. The birds flash by or sing high in the thick boughs of the pines. I enjoy birding but am not driven to identify every bird I hear or see. Sometimes I'm just plain lazy, and other times I'm satisfied with the pleasure of just listening to the woods full of musical sounds.

This time I stopped and scanned the nearby trees, and my eye stopped immediately at the bird that was broadcasting so loudly. It was obviously a warbler, but larger than most. The features that I first noticed were the bright pink legs and the yellow belly. When I managed to get my binoculars up, I could see that the head was greyish and the eyes were ringed in white and its back was brownish. It walked along a branch and imprinted its image in my mind.

I had just seen my first Connecticut warbler, and according to *The Life of Isle Royale* it is a rare summer resident.

* * *

It was going to be a long day's hike back to Windigo from Siskiwit Bay camp. Fourteen miles in all, and more than five miles, much of it going uphill, to reach the old fire tower on top of Feldtman Ridge. I hadn't bothered to do my morning stretching exercises, and within an hour my left Achilles tendon was complaining. I didn't look forward to limping all the way to Windigo, so I was focusing more on my discomfort than on the beauty around me as we neared a high open ridge.

Just as we approached a clearing, a raptor came swooping up from the far side of the hill and disappeared overhead. Soon another followed. I managed to come out of my self-indulgence quickly enough to look closely at the birds as they flew by. They were definitely falcons, as their long, pointed wings and narrow tails indicated, but they were slightly larger than kestrels and lacked the rust color on their backs.

Autumn mist fills the air and settles on fallen leaves that cover a trail on the Greenstone Ridge. (J. and A. Mahan)

My mind flashed "peregrine," but I then thought, no, they're not big enough.

They were merlins, falcons of the deep woods, the "pigeon hawk." While the peregrine uses cliffs and the kestrel relies on holes in hardwoods, this bird lives in holes in conifers, like those in the great marsh below the ridge. The merlin has a fast takeoff and will shoot up suddenly to alight on a tree or a cliff. It usually nests in dense stands and hunts open areas, like the bogs or cliff tops. According to *The Life of Isle Royale*, they are uncommon summer residents and rare as migrants. Another "lifer" for me.

I've often wished I could be a bird and feel the freedom of flight, and now with my aching ankle and more than ten miles yet to cover, I really envied those swift birds. They can easily travel at thirty miles per hour.

Later in the day, in a part of the forest that was burned in the 1930s, I saw a pair of pileated woodpeckers flying from tree to tree. I've seen pileateds before, yet it's a shock to see such big black birds go flapping by. Like the great blue heron, they remind me of prehistoric birds. Maybe it's the big, pointed crests of red feathers that stick out from the back of their heads, which reminds me of ancient soaring reptiles with bony crests and long, pointed snouts.

I watched the birds move in their slow undulating flight and finish with a sweep upward onto the side of a dead tree. Even from a distance, it's easy to see that they are big birds, much larger than any of the other woodpeckers. A pileated's wingspan extends twenty-seven to thirty inches, and its body is about eighteen inches long, very close in size to the common crow.

Braced by its tail against an old, dying tree, it pounds a slow, reverberating jackhammer noise. The drumming sound may advertise territory, call for a mate, or be the result of locating a meal in the rotting wood. The pileated makes oval or rectangular cavities, six inches or longer, in tree trunks, and on occasion actually chops down trees while eating. The leftover cavities can become merlin nests. On Isle Royale, where the full cycle of tree growth is unimpeded, they are permanent residents, although few in number.

* * *

The trail from Windigo to the Island Mine trail takes you through a beautiful stretch of sugar maple and yellow birch forest. Here the forest-dwelling birds fill the air with their melodious voices. The red-eyed vireos are plentiful in the tree tops and easy to pick out as they repeat "*veriee? veereo, veriee? veereo*" over and over again. The oven birds rustle the underbrush and call "*teacher, teacher, teacher,*" with increasing emphasis and volume with each couplet. The Swainson's thrush is more difficult. The lyrical flutelike notes mark it as a thrush, but it spirals a variety of whistles to a succession of ascending pitches. The really difficult songs to separate belong to the black-throated green and the black-throated blue warbler. The blues are more common than the greens in this woods, but they're both here.

The black-throated green tends to stay high in the upper branches, while the black-throated blue will occupy the middle to lower region. Both sing nasal songs that sound like they're saying "*zoo*" and "*zee*." It's the combination of the sounds and the intonation that differ. One phrase of the black-throated green is described in the field guides as a "dreamy, lisping '*zee zee zee zo zee*'" with the "*zo*" being a lower note. The black-throated blue's song is a slow series of "*zoo zoo zoo zee*," the "*zee*" ending on a higher pitch. It can be frustrating to try and learn songs that audition only a few weeks each year, but it is greatly rewarding and satisfying to see a bird with your mind that is hidden from your eye.

A wolf's howls are used to communicate many things within the pack. It is the lucky and infrequent camper who hears a chorus of howls on the island. (L. Rogers)

WOLVES AND MOOSE OF ISLE ROYALE

BY MIKE LINK

I turned the corner and stopped. There stood a moose, no more than ten feet away and looking twenty feet tall. It was startled. I was startled! I froze. It reacted. It gathered its wits and its gangly appendages into one brown mass that hurtled into the forest, while a clod of mud flew off its foot, sailed by my ear, and went "splat" on a birch tree. The moose was gone; its significance was not.

The moose of Isle Royale are legendary. There was the bull moose in rut that treed a photographer. It browsed within eyesight of the tree and hurried back to its base each time the photographer tried to descend. This continued until the moose got bored and moved on.

Then there were the two bull moose that fought outside Les and Fran Blacklock's honeymoon tent. The fight was so intense and close that the bull's legs kept brushing the canvas.

The essence of the island for me has always been moose—moose and wolves, with a smattering of beaver. Maybe it is bigness that attracts me, or maybe it is the drama of this predator/prey combination, land-locked on the same island, the hunter and the hunted, with nowhere else to go. Will the predator destroy its prey, as every wolf-hater claims? Will the slavering wolves destroy themselves through a gluttony of moose steaks?

The island is a biological reserve, because it is a representative north-woods boreal ecosystem and has had only minor ecological disturbances: a little fishing, mining, and logging, but nothing drastic, nothing that would change the composition of the island itself. Moose, beaver, and wolves had to migrate, along with the plants that support them, into lands left barren by the melting glaciers. We can't be sure when the moose arrived. We know from records of the voyageurs that moose were being slaughtered in the Superior region in the 1700s. Radisson and Groseilliers claimed to have killed six hundred in 1660 in just one spring hunt.

Moose were removed from Wisconsin and Michi-

gan by 1900. In 1934 and 1937, seventy-one moose were taken from Isle Royale and released on the Upper Peninsula of Michigan (a less than successful experiment). On the island, the moose had a mixed history. As the largest member of the deer family, it and its signs (track, scat, etc.) are too big to be totally inconspicuous, so reports in 1886 that no moose were seen or heard on the island should be fairly accurate accounts of the animal's population.

Olaus Murie, who was probably the greatest expert on mammals in the U.S., reported that the moose on Isle Royale had become scarce in 1880 and hunting "was probably sufficient to prevent the moose from becoming numerous or gaining a foothold." The 1905 Adams survey (University of Michigan) reported broken saplings that may have been made by feeding moose. In 1909, a survey of the island mammals produced a species list, and the moose was not on it.

In 1912, moose may have crossed the lake. That winter was so cold that the water froze solid between Isle Royale and the mainland, and some summer residents of the island believed that a large influx of moose made the remarkable journey over the frozen and uninviting icescape. Today, biologists question the ice crossing. Moose don't like to walk on ice. (Remember the deer on the ice in the movie *Bambi*? It was probably the only accurate part of the film.) Another theory is that they all swam in because they have been observed in Lake Superior halfway between Canada and Isle Royale. The idea of flotillas of moose immigrating from Canada challenges the imagination as much as the ice theory. To add to the complexity, the moose's rate of reproduction success is modest compared to the white-tailed deer's.

By 1930, there were reports of one thousand to three thousand moose on the island, but by 1936 there were an estimated two hundred. Why the crash? Apparently these herbivores had eaten themselves out of their home. There was no suitable habitat left.

Moose diet is diverse. In June they eat aquatic plants, diving if necessary, and rising to the surface to

In the summer months, moose search for succulent and nutritionally-rich water plants. (J. and A. Mahan)

present us with pictures of the big nose and bell dripping with water, waterlily root in mouth and flowers hanging limp beside the homely face. This is how they get sodium into their systems. In other months they eat woody plants and a variety of green herbaceous growth. For healthy moose, the island must present food in many different settings and seasons.

Park naturalist Bruce Weber notes that "a forest fire in 1936 affected 20% of the Island, causing vegetation to regenerate and presenting a banquet of birch and aspen that promoted increased moose reproduction in the late 1930's." The moose overate, they decimated their food supply, yet ten years later, the population was increasing! The island's ecology was teetering on the brink of a greater disaster—mass starvation of the moose, plus the elimination of parts of the plant community.

By 1949, a pack of wolves established themselves on Isle Royale. They probably did cross the ice, and they probably came in a single pack, or at least most of them did. They crossed fifteen to twenty miles of barren ice and arrived on an island with abundant food. They dined on moose and an occasional beaver. They established their territories and survived very

successfully.

The moose population went down, and the plants came back. As the wolves culled the weak, old, and diseased moose, and as they reduced pressure on the island's vegetation, their prey continued to reproduce. There was a tentative balance between predator and prey, one that existed without gun or trap. The wolves showed better "restraint" than humans.

The wolf pack increased in size into the 1970s, then split into four groups. The four packs divided the island; they fought for territory and dominance. Meanwhile, the moose kept eating and reproducing, and their population increased.

Eventually four packs became three, and then in 1987, the Harvey Lake pack was eliminated, leaving two competing packs to split the island. A research airplane witnessed the demise of one of the Harvey Lake pack in January 1987. The wolves were at a moose kill, resting, and the eastern pack was wandering in their territory when it discovered the kill. The eastern group paused very briefly about one hundred meters away from the resting wolves and the carcass, and then plunged into the deep snow in a frenzied attack on the alpha pair of Harvey Lake wolves. The fe-

Wolf pups are born in the spring. They stay near the den for the first few months and gradually extend their explorations to the world beyond. (L. Rogers)

male jumped up and avoided the conflict, but the alpha male was too slow and received the full brunt of the attack from the marauding wolves. He was pulled down and bloodied by repeated attacks and bites. The attackers clamped their jaws and hung on. After twelve minutes the alpha male still leaped up and counterattacked. The east pack made a brief retreat; then the Harvey Lake male was attacked once again, and after thirty minutes the three attackers walked away from his limp body.

It was a terrible struggle in the midst of what seemed like tremendous abundance, but in fact the wolf population had reached an all-time low since its discovery on the island in 1953. The 1987–88 population was down to a total of twelve wolves (with eight of them in two packs). Meanwhile, the moose increased to more than 1500.

The wolves, subject to high mortality rates, were dying out. Researchers wanted to know why. Three theories evolved. They did not include the idea that the wolves were killing each other just for the sake of killing. These were serious considerations. One thought was that the wolves might have contracted canine parvovirus, a disease of domestic dogs. The bi-

ologist's first examination of four wolves showed that two might have been exposed. The second possibility was that the wolves were dying because of their limited gene pool. Since there had been no new influx of wolves, they had only the genetic codes that they crossed the ice with originally, and the animals may have lost their genetic vitality. The third theory was that the moose, mostly young adults, were just too healthy and too hard to catch.

A big moose is too strong to be taken by the wolves. It is too formidable an opponent. The wolves had created a monster. By culling the herd, they had made it stronger and healthier, and now they were suffering. Unlike the wolf-haters' credo that wolves will destroy everything in sight, it turns out that the prey species might eat up its food stocks, but the predator usually can't.

The end of the story is in the future. The fate of the island may be another wandering pack, another moose die-off, or something we just can't predict at this time. The park remains a place of intense ecological interest, and the moose and wolf are still the strongest sirens for this ecologist.

Overleaf: Each fall, after the rut, the bull moose sheds his antlers. Slowly they become part of the island. (B. Firth)

81

The Pigeon River is a shared treasure that serves as a boundary between the U.S. and Canada. At the High Falls, the water roars over the rock edge and drops one hundred feet. (D. Braud)

THE PIGEON AND THE MINK

BY KATE CROWLEY

The noise from the waterfall was loud enough to make it difficult to hear one another when we were only fifteen feet apart, so Mike waved his arm, trying to get my attention. I picked my way carefully down the ice- and mud-covered slope, and as I got closer, I heard him say, "There's a mink down on the ice."

By the time I reached the edge of the precipice, the mink had disappeared back into a hole in the ice wall. As we waited, we watched water spurt out of holes in the sheet of ice that covered the rocks of Pigeon Falls.

The Pigeon River is a northern boundary, separating the United States and Canada. It is a large stream draining more than six hundred square miles. It originates in northern Cook County of Minnesota and flows east to Lake Superior—about sixty miles. Along the way it passes through many lakes, but the last twenty miles of the river are filled with drops of varying height, making it completely unnavigable, but beautiful in its force and fury.

It wasn't that long ago that logs were stopped at the lip of the falls and then sent shooting down a wooden sluiceway to the river below. Mike can remember visiting the falls as a child with his grandparents and witnessing the event. The graying trestle and trough still stand on the Canadian side of the river.

The falls we were looking at are also known as the High Falls, dropping almost one hundred feet. Because of the many lakes that empty into the Pigeon, it is a warm-water stream, with a good population of walleye and northern pike, which may have been one reason that the mink was living along its edge.

Mike and I and two of our children had stopped on the Canadian side of the border to hike back into the falls. A sign warned us that the trail was no longer maintained and that we traveled at our own risk. There was still snow on the trail, and it was a challenge to avoid the hidden channels of water that ran under the weakened crust.

At the river, a warm April sun glittered off the snow crystals and water. Gulls drifted on the current and lifted at our approach. We looked at a stone fireplace that stood alone in the dried grass and muddy ground.

Years ago a dancehall filled this spot, but now the music was made by rushing water and gull cries.

The sign was correct about the trail, it wasn't maintained; and we stepped carefully around the stretches of mud. A series of steep wooden steps led us up to the falls overlook. On the way, we passed the old sluiceway channel, with rusted sheets of metal still covering the rock walls.

The viewing area on the Canadian side is a parent's nightmare. The old railings and barriers have fallen, and you can walk right up to the edge of the crumbling precipice. Yet it did allow us to see down into the chasm of rushing, churning ice water.

On the other side of the river, Minnesota has built wooden platforms, at different levels, to allow people a safer viewing of the falls. We stared across at a young couple, who looked back at us from their sturdy viewpoint. Unfortunately, they couldn't see the mink show that we witnessed.

With constant reminders to the kids to be careful and not get too close to the edge, we watched the mink reemerge from its ice home and head down to the water (often a female mink will make its den near water). It stood looking down into the cold stream, ran a few feet forward along the ice, and peered in again. It appeared indecisive, like a bather trying to get up the nerve to make the plunge, but a wave splashed up and covered its face. That seemed to break the spell, and it dove in, a little too enthusiastically. Its long back arched over its head, and the mink somersaulted into the dark and turbulent water. Mink are very adept in the water, equipped with partially webbed feet and a thick, lustrous, dark-brown coat that acts like an insulating wetsuit.

We scanned the surface for a couple minutes before the mink popped up a few feet downstream from where it had entered. We couldn't see anything in its mouth, so if it had been fishing, it was apparently unsuccessful. Mink are carnivores and will eat just about anything that moves. In streams they catch fish and crayfish.

As soon as it hopped back onto the ice ledge, it began to stretch and rub its entire body on the snowy ground. As every good winter camper knows, snow is excellent at absorbing water from a soaking body. Then it scampered back up the ice hill and into its den.

Further along the edge of the cliff top, I spotted another mink. I called my family over, and we followed its progress along the rocks. We were too far away to guess its size, but it appeared slightly larger than the first one we had seen. Male mink measure 23 to 27.5 inches long, and females are slightly smaller. One third of the total body length is made of the bushy but tapering tail, tipped in black.

This mink was moving toward the falls, and we wondered whether it would swim across the river and find the other mink. They are solitary animals most of the year, except during the breeding season, which runs through March and April. A male may visit two or more females during these months; but any other time of year, a meeting between two adult mink results in violent conflict.

Neither of these mink seemed aware of the other, and the second one easily climbed up the rocks until it was almost eye level with us, and upwind, about fifty feet away. After a moment's hesitation, it disappeared into a hole in the hillside. Males have their own smaller dens.

A few days later, we saw another mink on the ice of the Brule River, in Judge C. R. Magney State Park. This one saw us at the same time and froze as we stared at one another. The mink's sight and hearing are less well developed than its sense of smell, and it may have been trying to figure out if we were a threat. This one had white streaks running down its throat and breast, which are normal variations in their coat colors. As we watched, it ran a few more feet and popped up behind an upturned ice block. Its shining black eyes focused hard on us, and then it silently slipped into the river.

Mink are still trapped for their fur, although most mink coats are produced from breeding farms. It is not surprising that they are wary of humans.

In just three days, we'd seen three wild mink. We had an opportunity to observe their movements and appearance, to see how they fit with the land—wild creatures living freely, in a still wild land.

Mink (L. D. Mech)

Kakabeka Falls is a remnant of its former self. The human urge to control and alter rivers has tamed and confined this cataract. (S. Kuchera)

ACROSS THE BORDER

BY MIKE LINK

It's funny what things stick in a person's memory. I have crossed the Pigeon River bridge dozens of times, yet the image I have is not a recent one. What I remember is a childhood vision of going to another country, of crossing the bridge, perhaps even on foot, and going to a Canadian store for a treat. It's hard to say what I bought; I was too enthralled with the Mountie in his red jacket and his hat to notice anything else. I have never had a more lasting childhood memory, I have never had the feeling of going to a foreign country like that one experience. Canada awakened a romantic image in my mind, and it has had a special allure ever since.

Sergeant Preston, dogsleds, wilderness, voyageurs, arctic rivers, Hudson's Bay, and English toffee — those are my symbols of Canada. Annually, my family would trek to Ontario, to the exotic cities of Port Arthur and Fort William, for the treasure of English toffee wrapped in bite-sized pieces and packaged in colorful tins.

I can't find the toffees anymore, but I am still struck by the Port and Fort image. Somewhere in my adulthood they merged, and Thunder Bay emerged, but the link between the big lake and the inland waters is still my strongest connection with the area.

Fort William was a Northwest Company post, the fort that followed Grand Portage when the American Fur Company exercised its political might and forced the Canadian company across the border. It was a mistake; the American Fur Company could not compete in the woodlands and lakes, and the Northwest Fur Company discovered that the Kaministikwia River was an even better entry point to the Northwest than the nine-mile portage.

It is appropriate that the fur industry was responsible for the founding of Thunder Bay. After all, it was responsible for the first settlements in Canada, and it was responsible for a history of conflict between two major industrial giants who raced across the top and bottom of the country in the pursuit of beavers. The Northwest and Hudson's Bay companies were shrewd industrialists with an army of the greatest wilderness travelers in history.

Fort William still stands. It disappeared for a while, but Canada brought it back into existence, and the life within and surrounding the walls of the fort are in the 1805 to 1815 time period. Walking among the stores and the various buildings is an experience that is truly existential. Conversations are about the 1800s, and they are carried on in the present, not the past, tense. The people within the fort speak as if Fraser, Thompson, and MacKenzie were still alive and making decisions. The cattle and chickens know no dates, so their lives cross time barriers easily; the tinsmiths, coopers, boat builders, and other artisans practice their crafts with great skill, and the visitor does well to read before entering in order to take advantage of the information that is available.

In a book that was published in 1850, titled *Lake Superior Its Physical Character, Vegetation, and Animals Compared with Those of Other and Similar Regions*, the great geologist Louis Agassiz described Fort William from his journey: "We now had before us a traverse of about fourteen miles to Fort William, the white buildings of which were visible amid the dark swamp across the bay . . . . The entrance of the river is wide and shallow, enclosing a large delta, cut through the middle by the stream, so that the river has in fact three mouths, the northern and southern ones some two or three miles apart. Some distance outside the mouth the water became very shoal, and islands were forming on which a few willows had already taken root.

"The river water is of the usual dark brown, and tolerably clear. The banks swampy, densely wooded, and lined with waterplants, among others the elegant heads of the sagittaria, also nuphar, equisetum, bullrushes, [sic]. Such was the luxuriance of the vegetation, that it reminded one of a swamp in the tropics, rather than of a northern river."

The fort that Agassiz found was "not very fashionable," the blockhouse was "falling to pieces," and the banquet hall was "burnt up for firewood." He added the comment that even the garden was "overgrown with weeds." But the river was still magnificent. He journeyed upstream to the famous Kakabeka Falls and the Portage de la Montagne. They took canoes, and a

At Fort William, history lives. Canoes like those used by the voyageurs are on display and occasionally put to use on the Kaministikwia River. (J. and A. Mahan)

competition formed between the craft, so that the paddles "looked like a row of tailors sewing against time." They soon arrived upstream at the falls.

Here is what Agassiz saw: " . . . guided by the roar of the fall, until we came out on an open grassy bank in front of it, and so near that we were drenched by the spray.

"From where we stood we could look up a long reach of the river, down which the stream comes foaming over a shallow bed, thrown up in jets of spray, like the rapids at Niagara. At the brink the stream is compressed, and tumbles over in two horseshoe-shaped falls, divided in the middle by a perpendicular chimney-like mass of rock some feet square, the upper part of which has been partly turned round on its base. The entire height of the fall is about one hundred and thirty feet, but somewhat filled up by fragments from above. Its breadth is about a hundred and fifty yards."

The river is not all free and wild anymore; the great falls of Kakabeka are overly developed with roads, walkways, vistas, and aids that are designed to enhance the natural experience. This is not the falls that the voyageur knew, it is not the glory of the wilderness like the High Falls of the Pigeon or many of the other beautiful drops on the rivers of Canada. It is treated like Niagara, robbed of its wildness, caged in construction, and needing space and freedom.

On the other end of the river, paper mills and industry affect the water quality. The port is threatened by the development that is made possible by the ideal location of the river and the protected bay. The city is in a conflict between preservation of heritage and the need for economic growth. There are nice parks within the city, the harbor is scenic, and the fort is magnificent; but the tinned toffees are gone, and so is some of the wildness.

SIBLEY PROVINCIAL PARK

Sibley Provincial Park is wild, it is rock and woods, on the horizon of Thunder Bay. It is the sleeping giant, Nanaboujou, the Indian spirit who is resting after helping to create the great lake. It is part of the land legend/land spirit of the north.

Sibley Provincial Park is located on a peninsula that juts out into Lake Superior. (J. and A. Mahan)

Endless horizons for the hiker. (S. Kuchera)

Agassiz called this Thunder Cape, and he had this description of it: "At a distance to the northward were two twin hills, called 'les mamelons,' by the voyageurs, and by the Indians, much more aptly, 'the knees'. One could easily fancy the rest of the gigantic body lying at ease on the plateau, with the head to the north, and the knees drawn up, in quiet contemplation of the sky; perhaps Nanaboujou, or the First Man."

Here I feel free. I can observe Pie Island, the Canadian Gibralter, and all the other islands that mark the bay's mouth, or I can walk into the forest and be enclosed in a boreal womb, tall-spired spruce and fir, elegant red and white pines, and smooth-barked aspens and birch.

Sibley is on a peninsula that contains the Sleeping Giant, as well as forest and lakes. This was the early home to Aqua-Plano Indians (*aqua* meaning water, *plano* meaning plains), who traveled along the retreating glacier to new hunting grounds and newly establishing ecology. They are believed to have been here about nine thousand years ago, and they might have used tools made of taconite, an iron ore, to hunt the big game that lived in the area at that time (for example, musk ox and caribou).

When they arrived, the quartzite cliffs that enticed my stepson Jon and me to climb and explore would have been fresh and shiny. The lichen growth would have been sparse, and the woody growth would have been very scattered. We climbed up fractured rock—ice-filled crevasses that may have been started by the weight of the glacier and then gradually widened by the melting and refreezing of water. Gradually the ice would wedge the rocks apart.

The wedges and the cracks became footholds for a forest that was climbing north in the shadow of the glacier. Today fir and spruce are very abundant, and the forest is dark and almost foreboding.

We were greeted by a pileated woodpecker that flew up by the road onto a large pine. It is part of the natural system at work in managing this park. The tree is infested with some insects that are taking advantage of a broken limb or some other entry point. The insects are killing the tree and converting it back to soil. The woodpecker is slowing the process of recycling by removing some of the insects and slowing down their feeding, but at the same time, it is helping by processing the nutrients of the insect and releasing them through its feces. Eventually, a heavy hitter like the pileated will weaken the tree by the holes that it is chopping, long rectangular openings that give access to carpenter ants.

Ichneuman wasps will land in these woodpecker holes and drill into the wood with their long hairlike ovipositors to lay eggs that will hatch and feast on the wood eaters. The tree meanwhile will grow, open new buds, produce more oxygen, and hold more nests. Its cones will feed the red squirrel, crossbills, chipmunks, and mice. Its needles will blanket the soil and then release acid in the fall rains, creating "pine tea," which will retard the growth of competitors.

Then a wind will blow, which stresses the trunk and sends the giant crashing to the ground. There it will lie, its thud lost in the sound absorption of the surrounding trees, and it will become an active participant in the cycle of soil, while the sun filters through the new opening and induces new growth. The variations are endless, the results are always positive. Letting nature be natural is the job of a park like this. It is the responsibility of the visitor to walk and ski and observe, to absorb the beauty and the reality of the lessons that are here.

Beyond the park is the old village of Silver Islet, a community that grew up around a silver mine that extended under the water from an island. The mine collapsed and the waters of Lake Superior filled the shaft, but the community retains the charm of another time. Unlike the older Fort William, this is not a park, nor are the people trying to relive the late 1800s.

The silver mine began in 1868 and produced a wealth of precious metal before it was closed in 1884. The owner and the lake waged a constant battle, but the eventual winner was obvious from the start.

Now the community is "picturesque," a dangerous word that often induces people to try to capitalize on the charm. The town is mostly made up of retired people, with an assayer's office, a wooden general store, and a boat dock that testify to busier times. Finnish and Swedish fishermen added their color to the scene. In its heyday, the community had more people than Thunder Bay, and many of the homes were floated across the bay to this site.

For us it was a chance to stretch, to watch blocks of ice float in the clear water, to see the sunlight reflected off the Trowbridge lighthouse, and to visit with some of the people. We couldn't have asked for anything more.

PERSPECTIVE

BY MIKE LINK

The North Shore, like Big Sur in California, is not a place so much as it is a combination of moods, places, seasons, water, rock, and forest. It's a magical part of Minnesota and Ontario. In a state where the Boundary Waters Canoe Area wears solitude, freedom, and wilderness, where the Mississippi grows from a quiet woodland stream to a brawling artery of the continent, Lake Superior is still the dominant single entity. In a province with the Quetico and James Bay, Lake Superior still lives up to its name.

It is more than a lake, it is a symbol of clean water on a polluted planet. It is its own weather system, and its tranquility is matched only by its fury. It is an inland port and an international waterway. Better that we call it a freshwater sea, because the word *lake* conjures too limited an image.

People who live by it, who work and play on it, who have visited it and spent time on the rocks that surround its waters, develop an emotional tie to the lake. Some close their eyes and see the white combers rolling across the rock reefs on a fogbound coast, some picture wind-whipped waves towering and surging up sheer rock faces to bathe the overhanging trees in water or ice. It is streaks of sunlight and dancing reflections, with a horizon that rolls off into infinity.

The shore is a magnet; it dominates your vision as roads bend around silver cliffs. Its sound is amplified by rolling cobblestones and exploding waves. The energy soothes the person in a tent, in a cabin, or on the shore. Its touch is cold and startling, even on the hottest day, and its taste is pure and refreshing. Unfortunately, sometimes taste and appearance can be deceiving.

Every other "great" lake has a warning label on the fishing license. On other waters, people are given quotas on the numbers of fish they should consume, because of the chemical brine that they live in. The oceans regurgitate the waste we put in them, and the restaurants must give surgeon-general warnings with the mussels and oysters. Only Superior maintains a quality catch, but we cannot afford complacency.

Erie became a cesspool, but recovered to meet moderate health standards. It has a flushing rate of decades. In Lake Superior, it will take centuries to replace the water that now resides in the basin. An average drop of rain is said to have a life of 191 years in the lake. I don't know how they followed the drops, but I know that it implies that what goes in, stays in.

Yet we let Reserve Mining dump tailings with asbestos fibers into the lake for decades. Towns and roads still allow salts and chemical to run off; the red clays of Wisconsin and Minnesota are loosened by people and eroded by runoff. Clays adhere to chemicals that fertilize lawns, kill insects, and destroy weeds.

Acid rain releases heavy metals into the watershed; ships discharge wastes; and Thunder Bay's river and harbor complex is so toxic that its fish are not edible. These practices are analogous to pouring poison into the ecosystem.

The lake is so big that each community can feel that its impact is negligible, but mathematics tells us that we must add the communities together and then multiply their impact by the number of steps in the system's ecological ladder.

PCBs and pesticides accompany the acid rains, and Lake Superior's tremendous size—350 miles by 160 miles, with a drainage basin of over 49,000 square miles—makes a large net to catch the fallout.

* * *

The lake entertains and transports us. But we need to take care of it. This is a land too special to let gradual degradation take place. The ruff has recently a entered the lake in the ballast of international vessels. Like the lamprey, this fish can seriously disrupt the lake's ecology, and we are the source of the problem. Likewise, we are responsible for the number of condominiums on the lakeshore, and the wooden platforms and railings on the once-wild Shovel Point.

We must make decisions on what is to be saved, and then we must watch those people whom we hire to protect those resources. But we cannot look to one government agency. We who love the lake and all of its shores must watch its health and speak out. This is a national treasure. It has what Aldo Leopold called "a sense of place."

There are few places that generate such a broad geographical, philosophical, and anthropological mix. Big Sur, Big Bend, the Blue Ridge, the Inland Passage—all have that big perspective, and each is a complex experience that each person must process, must define, for himself or herself.

We have seen the lake by car, foot, ski, snowshoe, canoe, sailboat, and climbing rope. It has been a place of research, work, and vacation. It is a flood of memories on a Precambrian palette, but it is also a part of our dedication to the protection of our planet.

ABOUT THE AUTHORS

Mike Link has an enthusiasm for adventures—adventures as diverse as paddling a wild river, sailing the open seas, observing a wild bird, keying out a new flower, or reading a good book. Each experience is a challenge, and each new assignment is an opportunity. Mike has two children, Matt and Julie, who have shared outdoor experiences with their father.

As director of Northwoods Audubon Center, Mike also is an instructor in outdoor education for Northland College and the University of Minnesota at Duluth. His published works include *Journeys To Door County*, *The Black Hills/Badlands*, *Outdoor Education*, and *Grazing*, and numerous magazine and newspaper articles.

Kate Crowley's skills as a naturalist and writer were developed during her nine years at the Minnesota Zoo, where she supervised the monorail interpretive program and wrote articles for zoo publications. Her knowledge of wildlife and wilderness grew with participation in volunteer bird censusing for the Minnesota River Valley Wildlife Refuge and exploration of wild lands in the U.S. and abroad. She has served for five years on the board of the Minnesota Naturalist Association.

Kate is the proud mother of Alyssa and Jonathon. Her interests include almost any outdoor activity, especially sailing and bird-watching and more recently, exploring her new home in Willow River, Minnesota, with Mike.

Mike and Kate were married aboard the ketch *Izmir* and sailed Lake Superior on their honeymoon. They are coauthors of a new series for Voyageur Press covering wildlife and wild lands.

(D. Cox)